The Way of The Garden

Spyros Geravelis

Table of Contents

About the Author

I was born and raised in Athens; however, from a young age, I was fortunate to spend all my summers on the Greek islands. I was not very social as a child (and I still am not), and I preferred to spend my days exploring the seabed with a mask and spearfishing, exploring the coast, or wandering through the pine forest rather than playing with other children. Under the sea or lost in the forest, I felt at home.

Architects and civil engineers dominated my family and social circle, and I grew up in an environment where aesthetics and art were important (my godfather was a professor at the School of Fine Arts, and art books were part of my childhood gifts). This nurtured in me a love for art. For as long as I can remember, I spent hours painting and listening to music, took painting and music lessons as a child, and art was always an important part of my life. It was also an environment dominated by a very Western mindset, disconnected from tradition, religion, and Greek heritage. Our interpretation of the world and life was dominated by rational thought and scientific understanding. I was always good at science subjects; they came easily to me, but I felt that this exhaustive analysis and fragmentation of things was a very elementary and incomplete tool for truly and wholly conceiving the world.

As I grew older, I became interested in religion. As a teenager and young man, I read books and explored religions and non-rational belief systems of people. I was fascinated by Chinese Taoism and Zen Buddhism—finally, not a dogmatic religion but a school of thought, a method, and a way of life for understanding the world freely and beyond the Procrustean bed of rational thought and science.

Meanwhile, I began studying at the Agricultural University of Thessaloniki (AUTH). Because of my two great loves, art and nature, I faced a big dilemma about what to study. Then, I discovered landscape architecture, which would allow me to combine my creative inclinations with my love of nature. So I went from painting landscapes I was seeing to bringing to life landscapes from my imagination that I had already drawn!

After completing my studies, I settled in Rhodes Island. Here, nature was abundant and easily accessible. I had not forgotten my love for the East; I have always been fascinated by Japanese aesthetics, philosophy, and art, as well as their gardens, and so I incorporated these into my work. I traveled to Japan, among other countries of the Orient; there, I spent most of my time immersed in the gardens of Kyoto and its surrounding countryside. I also had the unexpected fortune to meet, in the city where I live, a master of the arts with whom I studied internal martial arts, meditation, and the Art of Living for fifteen years.

This book is the result of my scientific education and 35 years of professional experience in urban green management and landscape design, my love for art and nature, as well as my engagement with Eastern philosophy and practices.

Acknowledgments

I would like to express my heartfelt appreciation to the visual artists whose work has added texture and depth to this book. Photos 4, 5, 6, and 7 feature the photographic work of Mizuno Katsuhiko, originally published in Invitation to Tea Gardens (1992, Mitsumura Suiko Shoin Co.), referenced on pages 1,3,6 and 10 of this book. While formal permission was not obtained, these images are credited with full respect for the original publication and artistic contribution. The atmospheric beauty and contemplative quality of Katsuhiko's photography resonate deeply with the book's themes and visual language.

The author's portrait was captured by Marializa Petropoulou, whose sensitive and expressive eye conveys more than an image; it captures the spirit of the words within. Her photographic contribution reflects a rare ability to mirror identity and emotion through the lens, and I am truly grateful for her generosity and collaboration.

To both artists, thank you for the creative inspiration your work brings. Your imagery has not merely complemented this project; it has become part of its voice.

Prologue

Modern civilization has increasingly distanced humans from nature, from one another, and even from their own inner selves. This disconnection has given rise to a superficial, consumption-driven way of life, fostering neuroses and a pervasive sense of meaninglessness. The Industrial Revolution deepened this rift, while advances in technology and the proliferation of mass media have transformed reality into mere representation—further severing individuals from authentic, embodied existence.

For over a century, analytical psychology has explored the consequences of this estrangement. Today, contemporary research in neurology, medicine, and mental health confirms the restorative effects of nature on the human psyche and body, identifying the specific natural elements that foster such healing. In traditional Eastern cultures, nature continues to be regarded as sacred and is experienced as such. The path to inner connection is often cultivated through time-honored spiritual and contemplative practices—a sensibility that is clearly reflected in the design of their gardens, particularly those of Japan, which are consciously crafted to embody these ideals.

For most urban dwellers, a garden or park may be their only consistent point of contact with the natural world. But what kind of garden can truly serve as a gateway to reconnecting not only with nature but also with the self? The healing potential of a garden lies in its ability to evoke tranquility, reverence, and spiritual connection—offering an almost initiatory experience of unity with the natural world.

By integrating insights from modern medicine, psychology, and landscape architecture with the timeless principles underlying Japanese garden design, we can uncover a set of

1

guiding principles for creating gardens that serve as spaces of reconnection—both with our internal world and the living environment around us. These gardens offer not only beauty but also a holistic approach to healing, reflection, and renewal.

Introduction

"Every time we touch nature, we are cleansed. People who have been tainted by excessive civilization take a walk in the forest or a bath in the sea. The bonds are cast off and they allow nature to touch them. This can happen from within or from the outside. Walking in the forest or lying on the grass, bathing in the sea is an entry into the unconscious from the outside. By immersing in ourselves through dreams, we touch nature from the inside. And this is the same thing; things are corrected and fall into their proper place."

Carl Jung, "Dream Analysis. Notes on a Lecture 1928-1930."

The garden and psychotherapy in the West and the East

A study involving 20,000 people conducted by the European Centre for Environment & Human Health at the University of Exeter found that individuals who spent two hours per week in green spaces—whether in local parks or other natural environments, all at once or over several visits—reported significantly better physical health and psychological well-being than those who did not. Interestingly, the study established that the two-hour threshold was crucial, with no observable benefits for those who did not meet it. These positive effects were consistent across different occupations, ethnic groups, and socioeconomic statuses, including people with chronic illnesses or disabilities.

In the West, there has been a profound disconnection from both nature and the inner self. We live in an artificially constructed environment—safe, comfortable, and increasingly removed from physical discomfort. The modern person rarely experiences basic bodily discomfort; we sit in cushioned chairs, sleep in comfortable beds, and use mechanical means to move from place to place. We have become dependent on technology and convenience, losing touch with fundamental physical activities such as sitting on the ground, an ability our bodies once knew well. Our relationship with nature (and with our own nature) has become distant, often uncomfortable, or even unreachable.

Concurrently, our perception of the world has been dominated by the rational, conscious mind, which tends to focus only on logical, linguistic processing. This superficial perspective overlooks the vast depth of our inner world, which, in truth, governs our existence. As Carl Jung pointed out, the four elements most repressed in the Western psyche are nature, animals, creative imagination, and the primal aspects of ourselves (which are often narrowly equated only with instinct and sexuality). Moreover, the spiritual dimension of the world has been largely stripped away. Nature has been reduced to an object for exploitation, devoid of meaning beyond its utilitarian value. While Freud's followers have recently begun to explore the psychological consequences of this alienation from nature, analytical psychologists like Jung have long recognized its detrimental effects on the psyche. Jung also spoke of the unconscious as the true core of the self. By disconnecting from it, we risk neuroses and a deep sense of emptiness. The Western overemphasis on rational thought and technological progress narrows our perception, leaving little space for the mysteries and untapped potentials of the unconscious mind.

As a result, we become alienated from the world in its entirety, both internal and external. Today, many of us struggle to sit with ourselves even for a few minutes. We reach for our phones at the slightest hint of boredom, seeking constant distraction without substance and preventing meaningful introspection. In this way, we have not only erased the spiritual dimension of the external world but have also lost touch with our inner lives, paving the way for various forms of neuroses.

In response to this alienation, the Western individual may turn to religious practices for spiritual renewal or psychotherapy for the analysis of the self. Psychotherapy seeks to bring unconscious material to the surface, allowing for the integration of these deeper, often hidden, aspects of the self into conscious awareness. This is how the Western world begins to approach the nature of the self from within.

However, engaging with nature from the outside—a direct, immersive experience—requires a different approach. It demands regular, sustained contact with the natural world, often at the cost of comfort or safety. For most, especially those in urban environments, accessing nature in a meaningful way can be difficult, if not impossible.

This is where the garden comes into play. I refer to the garden as a "gateway"—a hybrid space created by humans using elements of nature. The garden occupies a unique position, straddling both the natural and the artificial worlds. It embodies a balance between human control and nature's spontaneous forces. Here, contact with nature is accessible without requiring us to sacrifice our comfort or safety, offering an entry point to reconnect with the world around us. In this sense, the garden is a portal to the natural world, an accessible introduction to reconnection.

Historically, Western gardens evolved from the functional vegetable and herb gardens of the medieval period to the highly controlled, geometrically ordered landscapes of the Renaissance. These gardens reflected the Enlightenment's desire for rational order and mastery over nature. However, with the rise of Romanticism, gardens began to adopt a more naturalistic approach, particularly in England, where gardens sought to evoke the untamed beauty of nature, often incorporating mythological references. In this shift, a spiritual dimension returned to the garden.

In contrast, in the East—particularly in Japan and China—people have not lost their connection to either their inner worlds or the spiritual dimensions of nature. The Eastern approach, as I have personally explored in these cultures, is markedly different. In China, Taoism, and Japan's Shinto-Buddhism, there is a direct, experiential encounter with the cosmic unconscious, bypassing the conscious mind's analytical faculties. A Taoist teacher once said, "Those who know do not speak, and those who speak do not know." The Tao, meaning "the Way," is a method of aligning oneself with the universe—both within and without—an experience beyond the grasp of rational thought.

In Eastern thought, nature is imbued with sacredness and inhabited by spiritual beings—spirits not as romantic mythological remnants but as real, tangible entities. In Japan, for example, trees, rocks, and springs are believed to possess "kami," spirits of the ancient Shinto religion, which later integrated with Buddhism. I was particularly struck by the presence of Shinto shrines within Buddhist temples' gardens. This intertwining of nature and spirituality reflects a deep respect for the natural world as sacred. Throughout history, many cultures have recognized the existence of nature spirits—nymphs, satyrs, fairies—whose presence was felt as real by the people who lived in communion with nature.

In modern, Westernized Japan, the practice of "forest bathing" (shinrin-yoku) has become a popular form of preventive medicine. Westernization has taken a heavy toll on the Japanese psyche. The Japanese word for stress is… "Stress". So, the people of Japan are trying to find a new way back to their primordial relationship with nature. Since 2003, the Japanese government has invested over $4 million annually in research into the benefits of forest bathing. Despite Westernization's impact on Japanese society, this practice remains a potent means of reconnecting with nature. Florence Williams, in *The Nature Fix*, explains that forest bathing is about cultivating one's senses to be fully open to the natural world. It is not about wilderness but the unique blend of nature and civilization that the Japanese have cultivated over centuries.

In the West, nature is often approached with a mindset of control and exploitation, dissected to be analyzed, categorized, and ultimately commodified. In contrast, the Eastern approach is one of respect, admiration, and reverence—nature is sacred, a source of wisdom that cannot be fully understood by the rational mind alone. This is also true for the European Romantic, who, as William Blake said, "sees a world in a grain of sand and heaven in a wildflower."

The Japanese garden, far from merely imitating natural landscapes or pictorial representation, is a condensation of nature itself. It is a deeply spiritual act to create and experience such a garden—an act that transcends the material world. I would even argue that it is a religious act, though Taoism, Shinto, and Buddhism are not religions in the Western sense.

For the people of the East, the garden has long served as a space for spiritual growth and is of profound significance. The Japanese *Sakuteiki*, written over a thousand years ago, remains the oldest surviving treatise on garden design. Its focus is not on technical or aesthetic elements alone but on the allegorical and spiritual dimensions of the garden.

As psychoanalyst Joseph Henderson states, "Nature has lost its sacredness, but the spirit is uncertain and unsatisfied. Therefore, any real treatment of neurosis must awaken both spirit and nature to new life."

Thus, the psychotherapeutic power of the garden as a "gateway" lies in its ability to provide an experience of calm and respect, to imbue nature with sacredness, and to allow the natural world to enter our inner world. This experience cannot be forced by conscious effort; it must unfold naturally, like a psychoanalytic revelation or a religious enlightenment. In this sense, psychotherapy is not just about intellectual analysis but about a holistic experience of integrating the unconscious and spiritual aspects of existence. The garden, as a therapeutic space, offers a direct means of experiencing this process, bridging the conscious self with the deeper, unconscious, or spiritual dimensions of the psyche.

Let's not forget, after all, that the Paradise is a garden…

Creating Connection: The West

"The common suffering is the alienation from oneself, from one's fellow man, and from nature; the awareness that life runs out of one's hand like sand, and that one will die without having lived; that one lives in the midst of plenty and yet is joyless."

— Erich Fromm

The Industrial Revolution marked a profound rupture in the human relationship with both nature and the self. As populations flocked to massive urban centers, most found themselves absorbed in monotonous labor, disconnected from meaningful purpose, and alienated from the natural world. Consumerism reduced life's meaning to earning and spending, distracting us from any deeper sense of identity or fulfillment.

Mass media deepened this alienation by creating a hyperreal world of representations, replacing direct experience with curated images and narratives. In this "society of the spectacle," genuine human connection and a sense of internal coherence are lost. Reality is consumed through screens, and everything once directly lived becomes a simulation. As a mechanism of control, this spectacle promotes passive acceptance, endless consumption, and distraction from the true self.

In the digital age, our interaction with the world has shrunk to the confines of a 7-by-16 cm screen. This screen devours our attention with fleeting stimuli, replacing self-realization with the cultivation of a digital persona, making the path to personal and collective wholeness grow ever more obscure.

Connection with the Self

A genuine connection with the deep subconscious cannot be willed into being—it must arise organically. It often happens unexpectedly and while we are "busy doing other things." Achieving this connection requires a particular state of mind, one that quiets the conscious and opens space for intuitive, subconscious processes to unfold.

Psychoanalytic research underscores the importance of this mental state. Carl Jung, in particular, made significant contributions to understanding the connection to the unconscious. Unlike Freud, who focused largely on personal repressed material, Jung introduced the concept of the collective unconscious: a shared psychic inheritance composed of universal archetypes and symbols that shape human experience across cultures and generations.

Jung emphasized that access to the subconscious often comes through dreams, symbols, and creative expression—pathways that bypass the rational mind. These archetypal encounters, rooted in our evolutionary and cultural history, offer a bridge to our deeper selves.

In the West, psychoanalysis offers structured methods for engaging with the unconscious:

Free Association: Patients are encouraged to speak freely without censorship, allowing hidden thoughts and emotions to surface.

Dream Analysis: Dreams are seen as meaningful messages from the unconscious, rich in symbolism and latent content.

Transference: Emotional projections onto the therapist are explored as reflections of internal conflicts and unresolved relationships.

Yet even outside formal therapy, connection to the subconscious is fostered through states of relaxation and openness. Activities like meditation, hypnosis, and engaging in creative flow can loosen the grip of conscious thought and allow buried aspects of the psyche to emerge. Crucially, time in nature has proven to be a powerful catalyst for such states.

But art, too, has been offered as a means to fill the void of this lost connection—especially during the 20th century.

"From the promotion of the arts into 'Art' derives the most dominant myth concerning art: the myth of the absoluteness of the artist's activity.

In its earliest version, the myth treated art as an expression of human consciousness—a consciousness striving to understand itself... But the latest version of this myth presupposes a more complex, more tragic relationship between art and consciousness...

The modern myth enthrones, within the realm of art, many of the paradoxes implied by the attainment of that absolute state of being described by the great religious mystics."

— Susan Sontag, "The Aesthetics of Silence"

The art of the 20th century is characterized by a journey toward exploration and connection with the deep unconscious, influenced by the ideas of psychoanalysis, philosophy, and literature. Both artists and theorists developed new modes of expression to reveal the inner world. Through movements such as Expressionism, Surrealism, Dadaism, and, more directly, Abstract Expressionism, artists sought to investigate the uncharted territories of the subconscious.

Their goal was to move away from the conscious approach to art—both for the creator and the viewer (listener, reader)—

and to focus instead on personal, internal, and directly lived experiences.

The psychoanalysis of Freud and Jung opened new paths to understanding the human psyche and had a radical impact on art. The Surrealists were the first to incorporate techniques like automatic writing (André Breton) and dream imagery (Salvador Dalí) to bring the unconscious to the surface. Jung's notion of archetypes and the collective unconscious was reflected in artworks that highlighted the mysterious and the subconscious (Giorgio de Chirico).

Ultimately, Abstract Expressionism aims to express the unconscious without any mediation from the conscious mind— directly and often as a sudden shock. In Jackson Pollock's spontaneous painting process—where he would "enter" the canvas, pouring paint freely and randomly—mathematicians later discovered fractal structures similar to those found in nature and only recently revealed through mathematics.

Fractals are geometric shapes that exhibit self-similarity— patterns that repeat at different scales. One of the most famous examples is the Mandelbrot set, a mathematical visualization that shows infinite complexity and recurring patterns, no matter how deeply it is magnified. Mandelbrot found that many natural phenomena—clouds, coastlines, trees—are better described by fractal geometry than by traditional Euclidean forms.

It is revealing that a seemingly random, spontaneous, and arbitrary action by the artist—without conscious control—can expose natural structures and depict a deep reality that science has only recently uncovered with the help of advanced computational power.

Mandelbrot's equations were also consciously used by Iannis Xenakis in his musical compositions.

Susan Sontag argued that 20th-century art should be experienced not through the mediation of rational interpretation but through immediate sensory experience. According to Sontag, art is a medium through which we can touch the unexplored parts of ourselves. Rather than analysis and critique, which restrict art, she advocated for "interpretation through enjoyment," focusing on direct experience.

Connection with the Body

We sit only on chairs and sofas, sleep in comfortable beds, and move exclusively by mechanical means. We've become dependent on technology even for the simplest of actions, like sitting down and resting. Reconnecting with the body is essential for overall well-being, as it promotes deeper awareness of both physical sensations and emotional states.

There are established techniques that help restore our relationship with our bodies, such as:

- Physical Activity: Practices like yoga or dance enhance body awareness and connection.
- Sensory Rejuvenation: Massage, walks in nature, or enjoying different textures help us reconnect with bodily sensations.
- Mindfulness: Activities such as mindful walking heighten awareness of physical experiences.

Connecting with oneself and nature includes our relationship with the body—it is not a luxury but a vital necessity in a world that is increasingly distancing itself from the authentic human experience.

Connection with Nature

Biophilia

Biophilia is a term that describes the innate human tendency to seek connections with nature and other forms of life. While it was first introduced by psychoanalyst Erich Fromm in the 1960s, who defined it as "the passionate love of life and all that is alive," it was the American biologist Edward O. Wilson who further developed the idea in his 1984 book Biophilia. He proposed that humans have a genetic predisposition to connect with nature—a theory he called the "biophilia hypothesis."

The biophilia hypothesis suggests that humans are biologically programmed to bond with nature. This connection serves as a survival mechanism, helping early humans to locate resources and navigate their environments effectively. Wilson described biophilia as an emotional affinity with living organisms and ecosystems, which is crucial to human well-being. The inherent human attraction to natural environments means that people can achieve a spontaneous connection with nature, which can improve mental health and overall wellness. Research shows that interacting with nature can lead to lower stress levels, improved mood, and faster recovery from illness.

The idea of biophilic design has influenced architecture and urban planning, encouraging the integration of natural elements—such as plants, sunlight, and water features—into built environments to promote health and happiness.

Mental and Physical Health and Nature

Dr. Roger S. Ulrich is a leading researcher in the field of healthcare design, renowned for his influential studies on how the natural environment affects health.

Ulrich's research emphasizes the profound impact of nature on emotional responses, particularly on a subconscious level. His studies show that exposure to natural environments can trigger rapid emotional reactions that significantly support the achievement of a relaxed mental state.

He identifies physiological changes: exposure to nature leads to a reduced heart rate and lower levels of stress hormones such as cortisol and adrenaline. These changes suggest a shift toward a more relaxed state, which is crucial for recovery from stress. Ulrich found that emotional responses to natural stimuli can occur within milliseconds. The amygdala—a key brain region involved in processing emotions—is activated just 100 milliseconds after encountering natural stimuli.

His work is rooted in biophilic theory, which proposes that humans have evolved to respond positively to nature. Natural environments evoke feelings of safety and promote well-being, thereby supporting recovery processes in both body and mind.

Ulrich's 1984 study showed that surgical patients with a view of natural landscapes from their hospital windows experienced better recovery outcomes compared to those whose view was of a wall. Specifically, hospital stays were shorter: patients with a nature view stayed an average of 7.96 days, while those looking at a wall stayed 8.7 days. They also required less potent pain medication—often limited to aspirin or acetaminophen—and nurses' notes reported fewer negative comments regarding the condition of patients who had a view of nature.

Ulrich's research provides compelling evidence that nature elicits swift emotional responses on a subconscious level, facilitating recovery through physiological changes and positive emotional shifts.

Attention Restoration Theory (ART)

The Attention Restoration Theory (ART) was developed by psychologists Stephen and Rachel Kaplan in the late 1980s, during a time when growing engagement with indoor activities and technological advancements raised concerns about declining contact with nature. The theory posits that nature has restorative properties that help replenish mental energy and improve cognitive performance after periods of attention fatigue.

ART provides a framework for understanding how exposure to natural environments can facilitate mental restoration and enhance concentration. According to the theory, our mental resources—particularly attention—can become depleted due to the demands of modern life. ART emphasizes the importance of specific environmental features that promote effortless engagement or "soft fascination." These environments do not demand our attention but gently attract it, incorporating elements of mystery and encouraging exploration and reflection.

As our lives continue to grow more demanding, understanding and applying the principles of ART in our environments may be vital for maintaining mental well-being and cognitive functioning.

ART is based on four fundamental components:

Fascination: The effortless drawing of attention that nature can provoke. It is categorized into two types:

Soft Fascination: Gently engages individuals, allowing for reflection and introspection. Examples include watching leaves rustle in the wind or flowing water.

Hard Fascination: Captures attention through intense stimuli but does not offer the same restorative benefits as soft fascination.

Being Away: A mental state achieved when one is distanced from everyday stress and routine, allowing for a psychological "escape."

Extent: The perception of the breadth or scope of an environment, creating a sense of immersion in a different world that enhances the restorative experience.

Compatibility: How well an environment aligns with an individual's needs and activities, facilitating engagement without excessive demands.

These elements work together to create conditions favorable for mental restoration.

The Role of Soft Fascination

Soft fascination plays a central role in ART, engaging individuals without requiring their full attention. This type of involvement allows for the natural flow of thought and encourages exploration. For example, walking through a garden, one may be gently captivated by the subtle movements of nature—leaves swaying or birds flying—without feeling compelled to focus intensely on any single element. This gentle engagement fosters a state in which directed attention can rest and recover.

The Kaplans' theory highlights the value of environments that attract, rather than demand, attention. Engaging with soft fascination, people don't need to apply effortful concentration; instead, they are invited to explore at their own pace. This approach aligns with our innate preference for environments that inspire curiosity and exploration, prompting us to look "around the corner" rather than become fixed on specific stimuli.

The Element of Mystery

A key feature of a restorative environment is its ability to evoke a sense of mystery. Environments that do not immediately reveal all their interesting features—or that contain hidden elements—encourage people to explore further, fostering engagement and curiosity. For example, a winding path through a forest might lead to unexpected vistas or secluded clearings that invite further discovery. This element of surprise enhances concentration and mental restoration by providing stimuli for reflection and wonder.

Applications in Design

Incorporating ART principles into landscape design can significantly enhance mental well-being and foster a sense of connection with nature. Key design strategies include:

Keep it natural: Create a sense of "being away." Isolate the garden from surrounding artificial elements by creating visual and auditory barriers. Borrow natural views wherever possible and use natural elements and materials to evoke a strong sense of presence in nature.

Meandering paths into secluded areas: Not everything needs to be in plain view. This creates a sense of mystery, encourages exploration, and offers a variety of perspectives. Keep interesting features out of direct sight, allowing them to be discovered and inviting people to investigate further. This element of surprise supports cognitive restoration by providing opportunities for reflection and wonder. It also cultivates a sense of mystery.

Avoid features that demand attention: Dominant, spectacular elements that require focused viewing or are visible from afar interfere with the soft fascination process, diminishing therapeutic benefits by redirecting attention. Instead, support a state of mindfulness rather than directed attention.

Directed Attention vs. Mindfulness

Directed attention and mindfulness are two concepts with distinct characteristics and applications in cognitive processes and meditative practices.

Directed attention refers to the ability to focus on a specific stimulus or task while ignoring distractions. This form of attention is marked by:

Focused concentration: Directed attention involves focusing on a particular object or thought to enhance performance in tasks that require sustained attention.

Cognitive control: It requires active use of cognitive resources to maintain focus.

This type of attention is effortful and can become depleted over time.

Mindfulness, on the other hand, involves a broader awareness that includes relaxed attention and non-judgmental observation of experiences. It is a state of being fully present in the here and now, aware of one's thoughts, feelings, and sensations without judgment, interpretation, disapproval, or expectation. It is a form of awareness that embraces acceptance and attention to the present moment as it is without attempting to change it.

Interestingly, more than a century ago, a prominent landscape architect intuitively arrived at the same conclusions that the Kaplans would later confirm through scientific research.

Frederick Law Olmsted

"Gradually and silently, the charm takes hold of us; we know not exactly where or how."

—Frederick Law Olmsted

Frederick Law Olmsted (1822–1903) was a prominent American landscape architect widely recognized as the father of landscape architecture in the United States. Olmsted developed his own theory regarding the impact of landscape on the human psyche.

According to Olmsted, landscape operates through an unconscious process to produce relaxation and a "release" from mental functions strained by the noise and artificial environments of urban life. A necessary condition for such an experience is the absence of distractions and demands on conscious thought. The positive effect does not arise from examination, analysis, or comparison, nor from the appreciation of specific landscape features; it comes in a way that the viewer is unaware of its operation.

He contrasted the effect of a common wildflower on a hillside with that of an exotic imported hybrid of the same genus blooming under glass in a vase. The hybrid, he observed, would instantly draw attention, but "the former, though we passed it by without stopping, and though it did not interrupt our conversation or demand observation, may possibly, along with other objects of the same category, have touched us more deeply, come closer to us, and exerted a more soothing and revitalizing influence."

His desire to use landscape design to satisfy deep human needs rather than merely to create decorative spaces— combined with his belief that the process must be unconscious—led him to develop his own set of design principles, quite distinct from those of his contemporaries.

The "Spirit" of Place

Olmsted believed in respecting and utilizing the unique characteristics of a site, including its natural features and limitations. He argued that designs should be adapted to enhance the specific positive qualities of each location.

Unified Composition

All elements within a landscape should work harmoniously, with details subordinated to a central design goal. This approach ensures the landscape becomes organic and cohesive rather than simply decorative.

Orchestrated Movement

Olmsted's designs subtly guide movement through the landscape, creating pathways that separate different types of circulation (e.g., pedestrians and cyclists) to enhance safety and enjoyment.

Orchestrated Use

He advocated for a thoughtful arrangement of the various uses within a landscape, ensuring that each area serves its purpose without conflicting with others.

Accessibility and Democracy

Olmsted aimed to create inclusive public spaces that welcome people from all social backgrounds, promoting social interaction and community engagement.

Recreation and Relaxation

His designs included features that encouraged leisurely recreational activities, providing city dwellers with calm environments to escape the pressures of urban life.

Targeting the Unconscious

Olmsted sought to create landscapes that influence visitors on an unconscious level — much like music affects emotions without the need for conscious processing.

Avoiding Fashion for Fashion's Sake

He warned against the uncritical adoption of popular trends that might detract from a landscape's natural beauty and purpose, instead promoting timeless design principles.

Sustainable Design

Emphasizing environmental stewardship, Olmsted promoted the use of native plants and sustainable practices to ensure long-term ecological health and minimal maintenance.

Meeting Human Needs over Decoration

He believed the primary goal of landscape architecture should be to meet human needs, not just to create decorative art. This principle reflects his commitment to functional and health-promoting spaces.

We Are Made to Be Connected

Oliver Sacks, a renowned neurologist, deeply explored nature's psychological and physiological benefits in his writings. His essay "*Why We Need Gardens*," included in the collection *Everything in Its Place: First Loves and Last Tales*, expresses a profound connection between human well-being and the natural world.

Sacks returns to the concept of biophilia—the innate love for nature—which he argues is essential to the human experience. He maintained that this connection is not merely emotional but deeply rooted in our neurological makeup. In his observations, patients with severe neurological impairments often displayed remarkable abilities when engaged with nature, such as gardening. For example, he noted that individuals who struggled with basic bodily coordination could spontaneously plant seedlings when placed in a garden environment. This phenomenon reveals how nature can awaken fundamental human responses and capacities, leading to meaningful psychological healing.

Sacks described how gardens function as therapeutic spaces, offering a calming effect that can alleviate anxiety and distress. He found that interaction with nature could be more effective than medication for many of his patients suffering from chronic neurological conditions such as Alzheimer's and Parkinson's disease. The act of gardening—or simply being present in a green environment—allows people to reconnect with their senses and participate in meaningful activities.

Exposure to natural environments can result in physiological changes in the structure and function of the brain. Sacks observed that being in gardens or natural landscapes not only calmed his patients but also empowered them, enhancing their overall health. He discovered that nature's regenerative qualities could stimulate brain activity in ways that traditional therapies could not achieve.

In his reflections on nature, Sacks often recounted personal experiences that illustrated this bond. He described moments of awe while lying beneath ferns or visiting botanical gardens— experiences that deepened his sense of connection to something greater than himself.

Nature and Mindfulness

Choe, Jorgensen, and Sheffield have conducted important research on enhancing individuals' connection to nature. Their studies indicate that being in natural landscapes fosters a sense of *belonging* and emotional connection with the environment, which positively contributes to mental health. Their research emphasizes that *connection to nature*—the degree to which individuals feel they are part of the natural world—is a critical predictor of mental well-being.

Higher levels of connection with nature are associated with lower levels of stress, anxiety, and depression, suggesting that those who feel more connected to nature experience greater psychological benefits when exposed to natural environments. The studies found that activities conducted in natural settings significantly enhance both well-being and the sense of connectedness with nature. This relationship is mediated by feelings of *belonging* and *wholeness*, which are strengthened through direct experiences in nature. Exposure to nature has been linked to improvements in cognitive functioning and emotional well-being.

Their work also explores the role of *nature-based therapy*, which has shown improved mental health outcomes for individuals with psychological disorders. Their findings suggest that such therapies not only deepen connection with nature but also lead to significant reductions in symptoms of depression and anxiety.

The researchers examined how mindfulness practices are more effective when conducted in natural environments compared to urban or indoor settings. This suggests that the natural context can amplify the benefits of mindfulness on mental health, highlighting the importance of nature in psychotherapeutic interventions.

The findings of Choe, Jorgensen, and Sheffield support the integration of natural elements into urban design and therapeutic practices to promote better mental health outcomes.

Can We Measure Connection?

Connection with nature is more than just a physical interaction with the natural world—it reflects an emotional and cognitive bond that individuals feel toward it. This connection has, in fact, been made measurable through various scales, most notably the *Connectedness to Nature Scale* (CNS), which assesses how emotionally connected a person feels to nature. Research shows that individuals scoring higher on this scale tend to exhibit greater environmental awareness and engage in more sustainable behaviors.

To promote a deeper relationship with nature, several pathways have been identified:

Sensory Engagement: Encouraging individuals to focus on their senses while in natural environments enhances their appreciation of the surroundings.

Emotional Connection: Recognizing and expressing emotions related to nature can deepen the sense of connection.

Appreciation of Beauty: Observing the aesthetic qualities of nature can foster a sense of awe and belonging.

The *Connectedness to Nature Scale* (CNS), developed by Mayer and Frantz in 2004, was designed to measure individuals' emotional and experiential connection with the natural world. Originally composed of 14 items, subsequent studies refined it to 11 items that effectively capture the essence of this connection. The CNS reflects multiple dimensions of nature connectedness, with a particular focus on emotional and cognitive aspects. Key components of the scale include:

Sense of Unity: assesses feelings of oneness with nature, such as experiencing a sense of unity with the natural world.

Belonging to a Community: questions explore how individuals perceive themselves as part of a broader ecological community.

Recognition of Intelligence in Nature: measures appreciation for the intelligence and complexity of living organisms.

Affinity with Nature: The scale gauges feelings of kinship with animals and plants.

Awareness of Impact: Many items focus on understanding how personal actions affect the environment.

Belonging to the Earth: Participants reflect on their sense of belonging to the Earth and its ecosystems.

Interconnectedness: The scale captures feelings of being part of a larger web of life, emphasizing the interdependence of all living beings.

The *Connectedness to Nature Scale* is a widely used tool in research exploring human-nature relationships. It is effective in measuring both emotional and cognitive aspects of nature connectedness and is applicable across different cultural contexts, making it a valuable instrument for ecopsychologists and environmental researchers alike.

Hands in the Soil

Gardening is increasingly recognized for its psychological and health benefits, positively influencing both mental and physical well-being. This practice not only provides physical activity but also promotes wellness through various mechanisms.

Contact with soil can have beneficial effects on the immune system. Studies suggest that exposure to the rich microbial communities found in soil helps train the body's immune response, potentially reducing the risk of immune-related conditions such as asthma and allergies. Soil contact has also been linked to improvements in gut health. Microorganisms present in healthy soil can enhance gut microbiota diversity, which is crucial for digestion and overall health. A rich gut microbiome is associated with better metabolic function and reduced inflammation.

Gardening is also associated with significant reductions in stress and anxiety levels. Engaging in gardening activities allows individuals to focus on specific, tangible tasks, which can help relieve negative thoughts and emotions, leading to a calmer and more content mental state. Studies have shown that even brief interactions with gardening can improve mood and self-esteem, while longer gardening sessions provide deeper benefits. The act of nurturing plants from seed to harvest fosters a sense of pride and accomplishment. This process can enhance self-esteem; the visible results of gardening—healthy plants and vibrant gardens—serve as tangible proof of one's efforts, reinforcing positive self-esteem. Research also shows that gardening can improve cognitive functions such as attention span and memory retention. For children, involvement in gardening has been linked to better performance in attention-related tasks and improved recovery from stress. Moreover, the routine involved in gardening helps create structure, which can be beneficial for mental clarity and focus.

Therapeutic Applications

Horticultural therapy is emerging as a structured approach that uses gardening to address various mental health issues, including depression, anxiety, ADHD, and substance dependency. This form of therapy has shown lasting positive effects on participants' mental health, often extending beyond the duration of therapy sessions.

"*There are several reasons for the positive effects of gardening on well-being and mental health. First, there's the intense physical exertion that gardening activities demand. The benefits of physical activity and exercise for mental health are well established, with just 30 minutes of daily activity being enough to improve and maintain psychological well-being. Planting, weeding, digging, raking, and mowing are considered physically demanding tasks, and enthusiastic gardeners can easily expend as much energy as running or working out at the gym. Gardening offers a more creative and enjoyable way to get physical exercise and meet national exercise guidelines, which in turn support better psychological health. Gardening also allows individuals to interact with nature. In recent years, a growing number of studies conducted by researchers at the University of Essex have demonstrated the benefits of Green Exercise (G.E.—physical activity in natural settings or green spaces) on well-being and mental health, showing reductions in anxiety and depression, and increases in self-esteem, mood, and well-being across children and adolescents, adults, and vulnerable or disadvantaged populations. Even small doses, such as five minutes in nature, are considered beneficial for self-esteem and mood. Furthermore, gardening may provide greater benefits than physical activity or nature contact alone when it comes to promoting well-being and mental health. Thus, gardening offers an opportunity not only for interaction with nature but also for physical activity, thereby reaping all the health benefits of Green Exercise.*"

"Cultivating Wellbeing and Mental Health Through Gardening"

Vaithehy Shanmuganathan-Felton, Luke Felton, Celia Briseid, and Betty Maitland. Published in *The Psychologist*, journal of the British Psychological Society.

Connecting Spirit and Science

In his book *Gaia Alchemy: The Reuniting of Science, Soul, and Spirit*, Dr. Stephan Harding explores the integration of scientific interpretation with the psychological and spiritual dimensions of understanding the world. Drawing on James Lovelock's Gaia Theory, Harding examines how Earth functions as a self-regulating system where biological processes are interdependent. He advocates for viewing the planet as a living organism rather than a mere collection of inert matter. He presents a new narrative that seeks to reconnect humanity with the Earth, emphasizing the importance of perceiving nature as a living entity.

Harding argues that the separation of science and soul during the Scientific Revolution has led to a disconnection from nature. He supports the reunification of empirical science with insights from depth psychology to promote a holistic understanding of our relationship with Gaia.

Harding refers to the "Cartesian split" — the separation between mind and body, or the human soul and nature — which has characterized Western thought. Applying Jungian principles, he advocates for a holistic view that sees humans as part of a living Earth, emphasizing that psychological healing is intertwined with ecological awareness. Engaging with symbols and dreams, he suggests, can deepen our understanding of Gaia. This perspective encourages individuals to cultivate a deeper relationship with nature, recognizing it as an extension of their own soul.

Harding weaves Jung's depth psychology with the principles of alchemy to foster a deeper comprehension of our bond with the Earth. He sees parallels between the alchemical process and Jung's concept of individuation (as Jung himself first articulated), which is the journey toward self-realization and wholeness. Just as alchemy involves the transformation of base materials into gold, psychological transformation requires confronting and integrating parts of the self — including the shadow, those aspects of the psyche we often repress or ignore. Jungian psychology relies heavily on symbols and archetypes, universal patterns found in myths and dreams. Harding uses these concepts to show how nature communicates through symbolic imagery, proposing that engaging with these symbols can lead to both personal and collective healing. This symbolic exploration allows individuals to reconnect with their inner selves while simultaneously fostering a deeper bond with the natural world.

His message is about restoring a sense of a "sacred whole," which is vital for personal healing and the well-being of both individuals and the planet.

He also shares his own experiences and reflections, offering guided meditations and exercises aimed at enhancing one's receptivity to messages from the biosphere.

"A very common practice is what's called a sit spot, or as I call it, the Gaia Spot. I've had the same Gaia Spot for 27 years. That is, a place close to your home — it could be in your garden, but it's within nature — where you go regularly and just sit and observe and be in it. Simply watching a place as it changes through the seasons over time — hopefully for many years — allows you to develop a deep relationship with that place. The place then becomes a broader personality with which you relate, and of which you are an inseparable part. It stirs your imagination. I remember as a child, I wrote this little poem:

'Imagination was once the King,

Until television became everything.'"

— Stephan Harding

Creating Connection: The East

A Gateway to Enlightenment

"Only when your thoughts cease branching here and there—when you abandon all notions of seeking something, when your mind is as still as wood or stone—will you be on the right path to the Gate."

— Huang Po

The Japanese Garden

Japanese gardens have evolved over centuries, with their origins dating back to the Asuka period (6th–7th century CE). Influenced deeply by Chinese philosophies such as Taoism and Buddhism, these gardens developed as aesthetic arrangements of natural elements and also as spaces embodying philosophical and spiritual meaning.

There are many types of Japanese gardens, each with its own purpose and symbolism. Of particular spiritual significance are *Karesansui* (dry landscape gardens) and the Tea Garden, both of which reflect contemplative values rooted in Zen and traditional aesthetics. Alongside these, the *Sakuteiki*, a garden-making manual written a thousand years ago, remains one of the earliest and most influential texts in the history of landscape architecture.

In contemporary Japan, there is a growing movement to reclaim a sense of connection with nature, which has been increasingly lost through the process of Westernization. One notable practice that reflects this reconnection is *Shinrin-yoku*, or "forest bathing"—a meditative immersion in forest environments. The therapeutic benefits of Shinrin-yoku have been extensively researched, with scientists such as Miyazaki Yoshifumi and Qing Li demonstrating how forest exposure enhances both physical health and psychological well-being. Their work bridges traditional knowledge with modern science, positioning forest bathing as a legitimate therapeutic practice and offering valuable insights for the design of restorative landscapes.

Sakuteiki: The Spiritual Art of Garden Making

The *Sakuteiki*, or *Records of Garden Making*, is a foundational text in Japanese garden culture. Composed in the 11th century during the Heian period and traditionally attributed to the nobleman *Tachibana Toshitsuna*, the work offers more than practical guidelines—it presents a spiritual worldview where gardening becomes a path to inner harmony.

In *Sakuteiki*, the garden is envisioned as a microcosm of the universe. Each element—rock, water, and plant—is imbued with symbolic meaning and carefully placed according to natural principles and spiritual philosophy. The text outlines distinct design types—ocean, mountain stream, broad river, and marsh—each representing different aspects of the natural world and corresponding emotional states. This alignment of landscape form with human feeling reveals a deep understanding of the psychological and spiritual dimensions of space.

Central to *Sakuteiki* is the reverence for stones, seen as vessels of spiritual energy. Techniques for stone placement, known as *ishi wo taten koto* (the act of setting stones), are guided by respect for natural laws and the belief—rooted in Shinto traditions—that rocks house *kami* (spirits). This practice transforms gardening into a sacred ritual, where arranging stones becomes an invitation to presence, stillness, and contemplation.

The text also emphasizes the selection of native plants based on seasonal changes. This seasonal sensitivity promotes an intimate awareness of nature's rhythms and encourages the creation of gardens that evolve over time. In this way, the garden becomes a living calendar, reflecting impermanence and transition—key themes in Japanese culture and Zen philosophy.

Beyond form and technique, *Sakuteiki* explores the allegorical dimension of gardens. Every feature, from the meandering path to the placement of a stream, serves as a metaphor. The concept of *mono no aware* (acceptance of transience) and *wa* (harmony) permeates the design process, encouraging a deeper appreciation for the imperfect, the transient, and the natural. Gardening, thus, becomes an act of mindfulness—an art form where the external landscape mirrors and nurtures the internal.

Gardens as Spaces for Meditation

The gardens described in *Sakuteiki* are not meant for spectacle but for inward journeying. Unlike many Western gardens that prioritize visual complexity and abundance, Japanese gardens favor simplicity and subtlety. Dry gardens such as the Karesansui, with their raked sand and sparse compositions, symbolize fluidity and ephemerality. These features invite viewers into meditative awareness, echoing Zen principles where nature becomes a medium for spiritual insight. In this light, *Sakuteiki* transcends its role as a technical manual. It is a philosophical treatise, a spiritual guide, and an aesthetic manifesto. It offers a vision of garden-making that goes beyond beauty to cultivate presence, reflection, and connection—with nature, with the world, and with the self.

The enduring legacy of *Sakuteiki* lies in its invitation to create not just gardens but sanctuaries for the spirit. It reminds us that nature is not merely a backdrop to human life but a teacher, a mirror, and a companion on the path to inner peace and enlightenment. In a time when disconnection from the natural world has become commonplace, the values enshrined in *Sakuteiki* offer a timeless compass for restoring harmony— both within and without.

The Karesansui Garden

"Heaven, Earth, and I share the same root."

— Zen Master Sojo

The Karesansui gardens, also known as Japanese dry landscape gardens (often referred to in the West as "Zen gardens"), embody a unique synthesis of art, spirituality, and philosophy. More than carefully composed spaces, they are portals to reflection, mindfulness, and spiritual awakening. Emerging during the Kamakura and Muromachi periods (1185–1573), these gardens reflect the aesthetic principles of Zen Buddhism, emphasizing simplicity, tranquility, and a profound resonance with nature.

Unlike traditional gardens rich in vegetation and flowing water, Karesansui gardens use rocks, gravel, and sand to symbolize natural elements such as mountains, islands, and rivers. They are not designed merely to be admired but to be contemplated, serving as spaces for meditation and introspection.

To the Western visitor, a Karesansui garden can be an entirely unexpected experience—so much so that even the word *garden* may feel inadequate. The first impression is simultaneously soothing and disorienting. It can feel like a sudden jolt, a quiet slap that opens an unfamiliar dimension within. This confrontation with strangeness initiates a subtle cognitive dislocation, challenging habitual perceptions of reality and opening the door to a new way of seeing. One suddenly enters a world of stillness and timelessness, a monochrome universe echoing an essential reality—one that cannot be grasped through ordinary mental activity. As surface thoughts fall away, deeper inner responses are invited to emerge, untethered from the background noise of everyday life.

Zen Principles in Design

The design principles of Karesansui gardens are deeply rooted in Zen Buddhism, which emphasizes direct experience, mindfulness, and the pursuit of enlightenment through meditation. The minimalism of these gardens reflects these ideals, stripping away distraction and encouraging inward focus. The absence of lush vegetation or dynamic water elements draws attention to the subtle, abstract beauty of form, texture, and space.

Central to this aesthetic is the concept of wabi-sabi—the beauty of imperfection, transience, and simplicity. This principle teaches reverence for the natural aging of materials and an appreciation of what is modest, weathered, or incomplete. In the Karesansui garden, rocks may represent distant mountains or islands, while carefully raked gravel suggests rippling water. This abstraction is not meant to dictate a specific image but rather to engage the imagination of the viewer, prompting them to complete the landscape mentally. The activation of imagination is seen as a vital step toward spiritual awakening.

Symbols in Stillness

Every element in a Karesansui garden holds symbolic weight. Rocks stand with dignity and presence, exuding quiet strength and discipline. They symbolize stability amid life's impermanence and carry profound spiritual meaning, echoing the beliefs of both Shinto and Zen Buddhism. Rocks are not just aesthetic choices—they are living presences, seen in Shinto tradition as possible dwellings of the kami or spiritual beings. Their placement is deliberate, reflecting a deep respect for nature and its inherent rhythms.

Gravel, raked into flowing patterns that suggest waves or currents, represents the fluidity of life and the passage of time. These patterns are not fixed; they shift and get remade— echoing the impermanence of existence.

A central aspect of the garden's composition is the use of empty space or Ma. In Zen thought, Ma is not a void but a vital presence, a fullness within emptiness. The principle of yohaku-no-bi—the beauty of empty space—treats absence as an active element, equal in importance to physical form.

In Zen practice, emptiness (śūnyatā) is not merely the absence of things but a state of heightened awareness and clarity. It refers to the lack of inherent, separate existence in all phenomena—a realization that underlines the interconnectedness of all things and dissolves the illusion of the isolated self. Experiencing this emptiness, whether through deep meditation or sudden insight, can initially be disorienting or even frightening as it confronts the ego's habitual patterns. Yet, as one becomes familiar with it, a deeper sense of aliveness and awareness emerges.

A Space for Inner Stillness

Karesansui gardens are intended as spaces for meditation and silent contemplation. The act of raking the gravel into flowing patterns is not just maintenance—it is a form of moving meditation. Monks engage in this repetitive, mindful practice to still the mind and return to the present moment. This aligns with Zen principles of being fully awake to the now. Visitors to these gardens often report feelings of serenity and clarity. Removed from the noise and distractions of modern life, the environment encourages a reconnection with one's inner world. The garden's austere beauty evokes a sense of peace and introspection that can lead to self-discovery and spiritual clarity.

The emotional resonance of Karesansui Gardens is profound. Their minimalist design evokes a sense of eternity, a reverence for the sublime hidden within the imperfect. They echo the Zen experience of Mind—not the ordinary mind of chatter and conceptual thought, but the part of the self that connects with the universal mind, the deep substratum of awareness that connects all beings.

Karesansui gardens are not only spiritual spaces—they are also cultural monuments, reflecting Japan's enduring relationship with nature. Their influence has extended globally, inspiring landscape designers and architects to integrate Japanese aesthetics into Western contexts, even if only at the level of form.

Yet their true gift lies beyond form—in their ability to invite us inward toward stillness, clarity, and a renewed sense of presence.

1. *Karesansui* at *Ryoan-ji* Temple, one of Japan's most famous national monuments.

"In the garden of Ryoan-ji, you see no trees... A sweep of raked gravel and fifteen large, irregular stones compose it... Nothing, you might say, except the essential and the elemental. No pretension – and yet its power is overwhelming! The silent dignity, the bareness, and the austerity of these rocks suddenly open within you, like a strike from a sword, a dimension of depth; they whisper directly into the ear of the Formless Self the lesson of Emptiness..."

— Fotis Terzakis

2. *Karesansui* at Daisen-in, a sub-temple of Daitoku-ji — a temple of the Rinzai school of Zen and one of the most important Zen temples in Kyoto. The pinnacle of abstraction and empty space in garden design.

3. *Karesansui* at Ryōgen-in, another sub-temple of Daitoku-ji. The smallest *Karesansui* in Kyoto, it is also considered the oldest in Japan.

Experiencing Spirituality through Karesansui

Karesansui gardens embody profound spiritual and psychological elements rooted in Zen philosophy. Their minimalist design invites meditation while evoking emotional resonance through symbolic representations of nature's beauty. Each visitor's unique interpretation adds depth to these spaces—transforming them into personal sanctuaries for contemplation. As we navigate an increasingly complex world filled with distractions and noise, the experience of a *karesansui* garden offers a precious sense of serenity—a reminder to pause amidst the chaos and reconnect with our inner selves.

Through this exploration of the spirituality within these empty landscapes, there lies an opportunity for connection—not only on a personal level but collectively—as we strive for harmony between humanity and nature alike. Immersing ourselves in *karesansui* gardens cultivates a mindfulness that transcends mere observation; it becomes a path toward enlightenment. Mindfulness, which encourages full presence in the moment, is nurtured through the minimalist composition of these gardens, which strip away all distractions and challenge the mind to become still.

The Tea Garden

"The Tea Garden is intended to integrate natural and man-made materials in a way that reflects and contributes to our understanding of human consciousness... Rocks, plants, and water are used as simple materials by the artist to express distinctly human values. There is no attempt to represent nature as it is."

— *Invitation to Tea Gardens*, Preston L. Houser / Mizuno Katsuhiko

Japanese tea gardens, known as *roji*, serve as significant spaces that embody the essence of Japanese culture, spirituality, and aesthetics. These gardens are not mere landscapes; they are meticulously crafted environments designed to facilitate a unique experience that transcends the ordinary. The roots of the Japanese tea garden can be traced to the evolution of the tea ceremony, or *chanoyu*, which emerged during the Muromachi period (14th–16th centuries).

The Tea Ceremony (Chanoyu)

"As we hear the water flowing into the teacup, the dust of the mind is washed away."

— *Sen no Rikyū*

The Japanese tea ceremony, known as *chanoyu* or *chadō*, is a profound cultural practice that blends aesthetics, spiritual reflection, and social interaction—but more importantly, it serves as a ritual pathway toward enlightenment. It functions as a meditative practice that emphasizes harmony (*wa*), respect (*kei*), purity (*sei*), and tranquility (*jaku*)—principles deeply rooted in Zen Buddhism and connected to the Japanese notion of *Dō* (the Way). Considered the highest form of art, *chanoyu* requires many years of practice to master. Each movement performed during the ceremony is deliberate and full of meaning, creating a space where participants can connect deeply with themselves and their environment.

The tea ceremony is a form of meditation—a gateway to awakening. Participants engage in a precise sequence of actions that demand focus and presence, allowing them to detach from the chaos of everyday life and mental distraction. This meditative quality promotes a heightened awareness and a deep connection with the present moment, resonating with Zen teachings that emphasize living in the here and now. Before entering the ceremony, participants purify themselves both physically and spiritually. This ritual symbolizes releasing worldly distractions and emotional burdens, cultivating an atmosphere of inner peace. The act of preparing and serving tea becomes a ritual purification that fosters self-awareness and mental clarity.

The Japanese tea ceremony functions as a path toward enlightenment through Dō, the "Way" or path that guides individuals toward self-discovery and spiritual awakening. Dō reflects the philosophy of life as a continuous journey of inner refinement and mastery through the perfecting of an art. By engaging in this ritual, participants, through the refinement of the simple art of tea preparation, embark on a journey toward self-knowledge and harmony with the universe. They train for many years to perfect a sequence of simple gestures so that they may eventually be performed effortlessly, without conscious thought, allowing the self, the movement, and the environment to become one.

The Japanese tea ceremony transcends the simple act of preparing a beverage; it is a holistic practice that fosters spiritual growth and aims at connection with the Whole and personal self-realization. Grounded in the principles of Zen philosophy, it offers a sanctuary for contemplation, connection, and inner tranquility. And the garden plays a crucial role in the entire experience of the ceremony.

The Tea Garden (*roji*)

The tea garden is designed as a transitional space that prepares guests for the tea ceremony, allowing them to leave behind worldly concerns and enter a realm of tranquility and reflection. The term *roji* translates to "dewy path" and symbolizes a journey toward spiritual enlightenment. This concept is central to understanding the role of the garden as a boundary between the chaotic outside world and the serene, sacred space of the tea house. As guests walk along the *roji*, they engage in a meditative practice that promotes inner peace and self-awareness.

The layout of a tea garden typically consists of two main areas: the Outer Garden *(Soto-Roji)* and the Inner Garden *(Uchi-Roji)*. The Outer Garden serves as a zone of separation from the outside world, while the Inner Garden leads to the tea house itself. This distinction emphasizes the transition from daily life to a sacred space where one can experience calm and contemplation, moving from the mundane to the spiritual.

The tea garden is not merely a physical space; it is a bridge to inner serenity, a reminder that the path to enlightenment begins with simple, mindful steps.

4. The gate between the inner and outer garden, where the host welcomes the guest at *Mushanokoji Senke*, an important school of tea.

Photo: Mizuno Katsuhiko

5. The *tsukubai* at *Ura Senke*, another important school of tea.

Photo: Mizuno Katsuhiko

6. The entrance to the *roji* at *Omote Senke*, another important school of tea.

Photo: Mizuno Katsuhiko

7. The entrance to the Tea House at *Sento Gosho*, within the *Sento Imperial Palace* in Kyoto.

The Journey through the Tea Garden

Walking through a tea garden is an experience of mindfulness and contemplation. Guests begin their journey at a bamboo gate or a very low entrance that requires them to bow. As they proceed along the stepping stones—carefully placed to encourage awareness—they encounter various elements that invite reflection. These stepping stones, known in Japanese tea gardens as *tobi-ishi*, play a vital role in deepening the spiritual path of those participating in the tea ceremony (*chanoyu*). Walking on these stones demands guests to focus on each step, effectively grounding them in the present moment. This mindful movement allows them to shed daily concerns and mentally prepare for the upcoming ceremony.

As guests walk the path, they engage in a form of meditation that clears the mind and centers their thoughts. The simple act of moving from one stone to the next reinforces the transition, embodying the idea of progress toward spiritual enlightenment. The layout of the stepping stone paths restricts movement so that visitors walk in a single file rather than side by side. This promotes solitude and reflection during the journey through the garden. By limiting conversation and encouraging introspection, participants can immerse themselves in their thoughts and feelings as they approach the tea ceremony. This solitude is essential for spiritual preparation. It enables individuals to detach from daily life and enter a calm state of mind, which is necessary for fully appreciating the depth of the ritual.

The stepping stones are deliberately arranged in an irregular pattern to compel visitors to slow down and pay attention to their movement and surroundings. This irregularity contrasts with the straight, comfortable paths typically found in Western gardens, promoting a more contemplative experience. The path becomes a space for reflection, where guests can connect both with themselves and with nature.

The Way of The Garden

"The roji is the first stage of meditation—the passage to the state of enlightenment." — Kakuzō Okakura, The Book of Tea

Between the Outer Garden (*Soto-Roji*)—often designed with rocks or sand—and the Inner Garden (*Uchi-Roji*), which is greener, lies a simple wooden shelter, the *machiai*, a waiting area where guests sit on a bench until they are called. They then pass through a middle gate, the *naka kuguri*, which is typically low, requiring one to bow in order to enter. This act fosters a sense of humility essential for progressing toward the tea house. Within the inner garden, the visitor performs a cleansing ritual at the *tsukubai*, the wash basin area. Upon reaching it, the visitor must stop at a large stone, the *maeishi*, before the stone water basin, the *chozubachi*. The *chozubachi* is placed low to the ground so that one must bend down to reach it and perform the purification—a further act of humility. In Buddhist terms, washing the hands and mouth symbolizes a mind cleansed of illusion. After purification, the guest proceeds to the tea house. At this point, the walk through the garden should evoke a calm yet mindful stroll through a mountain forest. The garden's name, *"dewy path,"* is telling. Nature is usually covered in dew at dawn, which is considered by many the most magical time in nature. Relaxed, focused, and undistracted, the guest has already entered the illuminated world.

To quote from Preston L. Houser and Mizuno Katsuhiko's *Invitation to Tea Gardens*:

"Since the path through the garden takes precedence, the roji has become a profoundly symbolic environment for tea guests and practitioners alike. It has become a sacred space for a rite of passage with the deepest psychological significance—what C.G. Jung would call an archetype. An archetype is a system of psychological organization (myths, rituals, common dreams) participated in across generations as a way of preserving the mental health of the community."

Every element within a Japanese tea garden carries symbolic meaning that enhances the spiritual experience of the tea ceremony. Before entering the tea house, guests perform cleansing rituals at a *tsukubai*. Rocks represent stability and strength and carry deep symbolic and spiritual meaning. They serve not only as natural elements within the garden but also as symbols of nature's power, spiritual enlightenment, and pathways to inner peace.

The stepping stones act not only as physical paths but as spiritual ones leading toward enlightenment within the context of *chanoyu*. These *tobi-ishi* significantly influence the pace and mood of guests, enhancing the overall experience. The spacing and height of the stones are carefully considered when constructing a tea garden. There are specific types of arrangements and classifications of individual stones, each occupying varying degrees of importance—some playing unique roles in the ceremony. At the same time, the stones should never draw attention to themselves.

Their placement and spacing are critical in regulating how quickly guests move through the garden. Stones are set at varied intervals—some close together, others farther apart—slowing the pace of movement. This design forces guests to be mindful of their steps, fostering a more intentional and aware walking experience. This purposeful slowing down allows guests to more fully interact with their surroundings, helping to create a sense of anticipation and mindfulness as they transition to the tea house. The act of stepping from stone to stone becomes a meditative practice. Ultimately, these paths serve not only as physical routes but as internal journeys leading toward spiritual enlightenment.

Water symbolizes purity and transformation. The only water features are the *chozubachi* basins for purification rituals before entering the tea house. The spirit of the guest should not be distracted by ornate decorative elements.

Plant selection in the garden emphasizes the changing seasons, underscoring impermanence—a key concept in Zen Buddhism. There are no flowers or showy ornamental plants in a tea garden. The design invites guests to focus their attention on the subtle qualities of the tea garden and ceremony rather than on an intense visual experience, promoting a gentle elegance.

The minimalist design philosophy that governs Japanese gardens aligns with Zen principles such as *wabi-sabi*, which celebrates beauty in imperfection and simplicity. This aesthetic invites participants to find joy in understated elegance, to appreciate the small and simple things, and to deepen their spiritual connection during the ceremony.

The Tea House Experience

Tea houses (*chashitsu*) are typically small, often measuring just a few tatami mats in size. The architectural style of the *chashitsu* is commonly referred to as *sukiya-zukuri*, which emphasizes simplicity and harmony with nature. This style emerged in the late 15th century and is characterized by the use of natural materials such as wood, bamboo, clay, and thatched roofs. The layout generally includes two main areas: the *mizuya* (preparation area) and the main tea room where guests are served.

The entrance to the tea house, known as the *nijiriguchi* (Crawling-In Entrance), is a small door that requires guests to bend down or crawl to enter. This gesture symbolizes humility and equality among all participants, regardless of social status. A humble spirit is essential for entering a sacred space—both outwardly and inwardly. Upon entering the tea house, guests encounter an environment that promotes simplicity, tranquility, and harmony. The interior is covered with tatami and is empty, except for a *tokonoma*—an alcove or a shelf for displaying decorative items, typically a calligraphy scroll and a simple flower arrangement (*ikebana*) or even a single stone. Yes, even a simple stone is valued as a work of art and a subject of admiration. These elements are not merely decorative—they are essential components that contribute to the creation of a sacred atmosphere.

The act of serving and consuming tea is performed with deliberate mindfulness. Every movement is slow and intentional, reflecting Zen practices that promote calmness and awareness. The preparation of *matcha*—a powdered green tea—requires precision and focus. It is a series of formal, simple gestures practiced over many years to achieve perfection in every detail, transforming what could be an ordinary daily act into a profound ritual that embodies respect, purity, and harmony.

At its core, *chanoyu* is about mindfulness and enlightenment. The philosophy of *Ichigo Ichie*, meaning "one time, one meeting," emphasizes that every tea ceremony is unique and unrepeatable—just like every moment in life. This sentiment encourages participants to be fully present in the current experience rather than distracted by past regrets or future concerns. During the ceremony, both host and guests are invited to immerse themselves in every moment—appreciating not just the taste of the tea but also the beauty of the simple object displayed in the *tokonoma*, the utensils used for serving the tea (which are works of art in their own right), and the execution of the ritual gestures. This practice cultivates a sense of connection not only between individuals but also with their inner self, the environment, and nature itself—creating spiritual bonds that transcend individual existence and lead toward enlightenment.

And the garden is an inseparable part of this experience. The Tea Garden and *chanoyu* remind us that true beauty lies in simplicity, true serenity in humility, and true enlightenment in deep connection with each moment.

The West Meets the East

Carl G. Jung

"Even a superficial acquaintance with Eastern thought is enough to reveal that a fundamental difference separates the East from the West... Christian Western thought sees the human being as entirely dependent on the grace of God... The East, however, insists that the individual is solely responsible for their higher development, as it believes in 'self-liberation.'"

—Carl G. Jung

I first encountered Carl Jung through his forewords to the *I Ching* and the Tibetan *Book of the Dead* (*Bardo Thodol*). These texts were, in fact, the starting point that led me to read about depth psychology and psychoanalysis.

Jung's extensive engagement with Eastern philosophy and its practices significantly shaped his analytical psychology. He approached these traditions through a psychoanalytic lens, often highlighting the differences between the spiritual paradigms of East and West. His dialogue with Eastern religious traditions spanned nearly fifty years and profoundly influenced his theoretical framework. He saw these traditions as essential for critiquing and expanding Western psychological concepts, arguing that Western consciousness is historically and geographically limited. He believed that integrating Eastern psychology could offer valuable insights into the collective unconscious and the archetypes that shape human psychic experience.

Jung had a particular interest in Buddhism, seeing it not as a religion but as a psychological phenomenon. He appreciated its capacity for "reforming thought," which he believed could offer important psychological truths when stripped of its religious context. Despite acknowledging its value, Jung warned Westerners not to practice Buddhism as a religion, arguing that they lacked the necessary cultural and psychological foundations to effectively engage with its deeper dimensions. He emphasized practices such as introspection and meditation—methods that resonate with Eastern techniques aimed at self-realization. Jung believed that such practices could facilitate the integration of the conscious and unconscious self, echoing the focus of Eastern philosophies on achieving inner harmony. Jung asserted that there is an inherent incompatibility between the East's spiritual introversion and the West's spiritual extraversion. He argued that the historical and cultural contexts of these traditions have led to fundamentally different approaches to spirituality.

His exploration of Eastern philosophy was marked by both respect and caution. He acknowledged the deep wisdom these traditions could offer but also emphasized the challenges Westerners face when trying to adopt them without understanding their cultural roots. His work continues to serve as a bridge between these diverse psychological landscapes, encouraging a dialogue that honors the unique contributions of both traditions to our understanding of the human soul.

Erich Fromm

Erich Fromm, a prominent psychoanalyst and social philosopher, explored the connections between Zen Buddhism and psychoanalysis, particularly in his 1960 book *Zen Buddhism and Psychoanalysis*, which he co-authored. His work emphasizes the shared goal of both approaches: the liberation of the self through heightened awareness. Fromm argues that both Zen and psychoanalysis aim to make the unconscious conscious, thus promoting self-knowledge. He maintains that this heightened awareness leads to a realization of the individual's potential for love and kindness rather than a regression into a more primitive state. This transformative process

58

is akin to achieving enlightenment in Zen, known as *satori*. Both practices encourage individuals to confront their unconscious thoughts and emotions.

Fromm believed that understanding the self is crucial for personal development and the well-being of society. The ultimate aim of both psychoanalysis and Zen is to achieve freedom through understanding the true nature of the self. He contended that this understanding liberates individuals from imaginary mental constructs that hinder authentic living. Fromm was critical of Western rationalism, which he viewed as limiting human potential. He proposed that traditional psychoanalysis often neglects spiritual dimensions, advocating for a more holistic approach that incorporates insights from Zen Buddhism. He regarded Zen as a path to deep psychological transformation, aligned with his humanistic philosophy, which emphasizes character development beyond instinctual drives. Fromm's exploration of Zen within the context of psychoanalysis highlights a profound link between self-awareness and liberation. By integrating insights from both traditions, he proposed a more comprehensive understanding of human psychology that transcends traditional limitations and promotes a path toward enlightenment and personal fulfillment. His work remains influential in contemporary discussions on the interaction between spirituality and psychology.

It was the book *Zen in the Art of Archery* that introduced Zen practice to a wider Western audience. This work, authored by German philosopher Eugen Herrigel and published in 1948, explores the intersection of Zen Buddhism and the practice of archery—specifically *Kyūdō*, the Japanese art of archery, another *Do* or "way" to enlightenment. Herrigel's journey began when he moved to Japan in the 1920s and sought to understand Zen through the practice of archery under a master named Awa Kenzo. Herrigel's book is not a manual on archery; rather, it serves as a philosophical exploration of self-awareness and self-mastery as pursued through the Japanese concept of

Do (path or way). He describes his two-year apprenticeship, during which he learned that true mastery in archery goes beyond physical skill. Instead, it requires a deep mental state in which the archer becomes one with the act of shooting—"the shooter and the target"—achieving a state of "aimless action" or "artless art." This process emphasizes liberation from self-consciousness in order to attain a profound connection between bow and arrow, self and universe.

Since then, Eastern practices have become a significant part of Western pursuits of healing and well-being. Yoga, meditation, and internal martial arts—which combine physical movement with spiritual development—are now widely practiced and appreciated, though often stripped of their deeper spiritual foundations.

In the field of landscape architecture, Japanese gardens have also profoundly influenced the West. The introduction of Japanese gardens to the West can be traced back to the late 19th century when Japan opened itself to international influences during the Meiji period. This era saw a growing admiration for all things Japanese, leading to the incorporation of Japanese garden elements into Western landscapes. We've all seen Claude Monet's paintings of his Japanese-style garden. Monet's gardens in Giverny were deeply influenced by the aesthetics of Japanese gardens. His love for Japan began in the late 19th century, encouraged by his collection of *ukiyo-e* woodblock prints and the broader cultural fascination with Japanese art following the 1867 World Exposition, where Japan had a significant presence.

Since then, Japanese gardens have been built across the Western world, with their elements integrated into and profoundly influencing landscape architecture aesthetics.

Shinrin-yoku (Forest Bathing)

Yoshifumi Miyazaki is a leading figure in research surrounding *Shinrin-yoku*, or forest bathing—a practice originating from Japan that emphasizes the health benefits of immersion in forest environments. His work has significantly contributed to our understanding of how exposure to forests can enhance both physical and psychological well-being.

Shinrin-yoku, which translates as "forest bathing," gained popularity in Japan during the 1980s as a therapeutic practice aimed at improving health through nature immersion. This practice is based on the belief that spending time in forests can reduce stress, elevate mood, and strengthen the immune system. It involves engaging with nature through all five senses, promoting a holistic experience that fosters relaxation and recovery from daily pressures.

In modern, westernized Japan, forest bathing is a recognized preventive healthcare practice. Since 2003, the Japanese government has allocated $4 million annually for research into the practice. Miyazaki emphasizes that *Shinrin-yoku* is not merely a therapeutic technique but is deeply rooted in cultural traditions in Japanese society, with origins traceable to the country's Buddhist and Shinto heritage. These beliefs highlight a profound connection to nature, viewing forests as sacred spaces inhabited by *kami* (spirits) that foster spiritual healing and communal well-being. The practice reflects a long-standing relationship between people and nature, advocating a lifestyle in harmony with natural surroundings.

Miyazaki's studies have demonstrated various health benefits associated with *Shinrin-yoku*:

Improved Cardiovascular Function: Regular exposure to forest environments is linked to enhanced cardiovascular health and better hemodynamic responses.

Enhanced Immune Function: Forest bathing can boost the activity of natural killer (NK) cells, which play a critical role in the body's immune defense.

Stress and Anxiety Reduction: Participants in forest bathing activities report lower cortisol levels—a key stress hormone—leading to improved emotional states and reduced anxiety.

Miyazaki's research also identifies specific environmental characteristics that significantly amplify the therapeutic effects of forest bathing. These include:

Biodiversity: Rich biodiversity in flora and fauna enhances sensory engagement. Forests with a variety of tree, plant, and animal species offer a richer experience, allowing individuals to connect deeply with their surroundings through sight, sound, and smell.

Natural Aromas: The presence of phytoncides—natural compounds emitted by trees—plays a crucial role. These not only have antimicrobial properties but also promote relaxation and support immune function, acting as a form of natural aromatherapy that reduces stress and improves mood.

Soothing Sounds: Calming natural sounds, like rustling leaves, flowing water, and birdcalls, contribute to a serene atmosphere. These auditory elements support mindfulness and enrich the experience of being present in nature.

Accessibility: Easily accessible locations encourage participation in forest bathing. Areas reachable by public transport or a short walk enable more people to enjoy its benefits.

Well-Maintained Trails: Properly maintained paths facilitate exploration while ensuring safety. Trails should encourage slow walking and careful observation of nature, which are central to *Shinrin-yoku*.

Seasonal Variation: Sites that change with the seasons offer diverse experiences throughout the year, allowing participants to enjoy and interact with different aspects of nature.

Cultural Significance: Places with cultural or historical importance can deepen the connection to the land and enhance the experience by offering additional layers of meaning.

Solitude and Peace: A quiet environment free from urban noise and distractions is essential. Locations that offer solitude allow individuals to fully relax and engage in self-reflection or mindfulness practices.

These environmental features collectively create an ideal setting for forest bathing, enhancing its therapeutic effects on mental and physical health while fostering a deeper connection with nature.

Landscape design elements based on Shinrin-yoku research

Based on Miyazaki's work, we can extract key design principles to strengthen the connection to nature within built landscapes:

Keep It Natural

Use natural elements and materials for paths and amenities. Whenever possible, opt for natural features over artificial ones—e.g., using a rock or a tree trunk as a bench. Trails and overall layout should mimic natural flow, with smooth transitions between spaces.

Plant Life

Use native plants to enhance biodiversity and ecological resilience. Plant in layered vegetation along the trails to mimic natural ecosystems—this may include ground covers, herbs, shrubs, and tall trees. Organize plants in groupings as they appear in the wild.

Engage All the Senses

Sensory engagement in natural environments boosts awareness and appreciation of the surroundings. This includes focusing on what we can see, hear, smell, touch, and taste. By tuning into these inputs, we create a deeper, synchronized connection with nature—going beyond seeing nature as a mere background.

VISION

Humans primarily rely on visual information to understand environmental structure. Visual memory is distinct from other forms and has a remarkable capacity for detail retention.

Fractality

Fractality refers to a geometric condition where a pattern repeats at various scales. Fractal shapes are known for their self-similarity—parts resemble the whole at any zoom level. Nature is inherently fractal, and we should aim to preserve this quality in landscape design.

Richard E. Taylor, a Nobel laureate physicist, made major contributions to our understanding of fractals and their effects on human perception and neurological responses. His interdisciplinary research explored the relationship between natural fractal patterns and physiological responses, especially in terms of eye movement and brain activity.

Taylor's work reveals the beauty of fractals in nature and their significance in shaping human perception and brain function. His findings suggest therapeutic potential through art, design principles, and cognitive understanding.

Fractals appear in many natural phenomena, such as:

Trees: Branches exhibit fractal geometry, with each dividing into smaller ones in a repeating pattern.

Rivers: Tributaries flowing into a main river mimic fractal structures through complex branching.

Clouds & Mountains: Both show fractal features, with similar forms appearing regardless of observation scale.

These patterns are not only aesthetically pleasing—they serve functional roles in nature, such as optimizing resource distribution or facilitating efficient movement.

Eye Movement and Fractals

Taylor's research explored how people interact with fractal stimuli through eye movements. Observing fractal images, our eyes follow specific paths that mirror the fractal structure, thanks to the visual system's design optimized for processing such patterns.

Studies show that eye movements when viewing fractals often follow fractal paths—similar to the foraging patterns seen in animals like birds.

Neurological Effects: Taylor's experiments using eye-tracking and brain imaging (EEG and fMRI) revealed that viewing fractals can reduce stress levels by up to 60%, pointing to a physiological match between the viewer's visual system, mental state, and the fractal structure.

Fractals stimulate brain areas related to emotion and memory. This suggests that our attraction to these patterns may stem from evolutionary advantages, promoting calmness and enhancing cognitive processing.

Fractality in Landscape Design

Repetition: Repeat patterns across scales.

Fibonacci Sequence: Use this for spacing and arranging plants.

Spirals: Incorporate spiral shapes that mimic natural forms.

Path Design: Create gently curving paths that branch like tree limbs to evoke an organic feel and encourage exploration.

Repetitive Patterns: Along paths, use plant clusters or stone arrangements to create harmony and visual continuity.

Natural Elements: Use materials that reflect natural patterns, like stones in fractal formations or gravel paths mimicking river flows.

Fractal Growth Plants: Plant species with visible fractal growth patterns to reinforce the design concept.

Layered Vegetation: Plant multiple vegetation layers along paths to mimic natural ecosystems—ground covers, shrubs, and tall trees in self-similar structures.

Color and Texture: Select plants with varied but complementary colors and textures. Repetition of colors can visually echo fractal motifs.

SMELL

Our noses can detect a trillion scents, and, more importantly, smell connects directly to the primal brain—the amygdala—which is linked to the hippocampus, where memories are stored. Scents impact our emotions more powerfully and directly than any other sense, often subconsciously. Scents have deep psychological effects and can also benefit health.

Dr. Qing Li, a student of Miyazaki Yoshifumi, is a leading figure in forest medicine. He has conducted extensive research on the benefits of staying in natural, especially forested, environments. His work focuses on *Shinrin-yoku* and the role of phytoncides—natural oils emitted by trees and plants.

These compounds are defense mechanisms for trees against pests and diseases. Human exposure to them offers proven health benefits, such as:

Stress Reduction: Phytoncides help lower levels of stress hormones like cortisol, adrenaline, and noradrenaline.

Immune System Boost: Research shows that phytoncides increase the activity of NK cells that target and destroy virus-infected and cancerous cells.

Lavender and rosemary, for example, are well-known for their calming properties—supported by scientific studies and traditional aromatherapy.

Lavender essential oil contains compounds such as linalool and linalyl acetate, both known for their calming properties. These compounds interact with the brain's limbic system, influencing emotions and promoting feelings of calmness and relaxation. Research shows that inhaling lavender can lower heart rate and blood pressure, offering a natural sense of relaxation. Furthermore, lavender has been shown to enhance the production of serotonin—a neurotransmitter responsible for regulating mood and reducing anxiety.

Rosemary essential oil is also known for its positive effects on mood and cognitive function. It contains active compounds like alpha-pinene, which help lower levels of corticosterone—a hormone linked to stress. Studies indicate that inhaling rosemary can boost memory performance and improve outcomes in stressful situations, such as during exams. The stimulating effects of rosemary are associated with its ability to increase dopamine release in the brain, enhancing both mood and cognitive function.

HEARING

When was the last time you truly heard the sound of silence? If you're young, perhaps you never have. Unfortunately, silence is disappearing. Gordon Hempton, an acoustic ecologist and founder of Quiet Parks International—a nonprofit that certifies noise-free zones—states:

'The systematic disappearance of quiet places continues because they were never officially recognized in the 40 years I've been searching for them to do my work as a sound researcher. Ten years ago, there were twelve quiet places in the United States. Today, I estimate there are about eight."

"Silence is not the absence of sound, but the absence of noise pollution. I define noise pollution as the presence of relatively loud, low-value sounds that rob us of access to subtler, lower-volume, high-value sounds. The number one source of noise pollution is transportation."

Twenty to thirty years ago, we believed we had to protect our hearing from loud noises to avoid hearing loss. Today, we know that even lower-level sounds—below the threshold of hearing damage—can increase the risk of cardiovascular disease.

Noise pollution has serious health consequences. Studies show that chronic exposure to noise can lead to cardiovascular disorders, anxiety-related conditions, and diminished cognitive performance in children. Soundscapes—including natural sounds (biophony), geological sounds (geophony), and human-made sounds (anthrophony)—reflect the health of ecosystems and our connection to them. Preserving silence is vital to sustaining natural environments.

Hempton describes Earth as a "solar-powered jukebox" because natural environments are rich with musical qualities we can experience through careful listening. He invites us to connect with nature not only visually but also through sound—recognizing the beauty and complexity of natural acoustics. A garden rich in plant biodiversity will attract wildlife and their therapeutic sounds, primarily birds and insects, providing them with food and shelter. A water element, even a small pond with a waterfall, can have a powerful auditory effect as a natural background sound.

Research increasingly highlights the therapeutic benefits of nature sounds, showing their ability to reduce stress, improve mood, and promote general well-being through neurological and physiological mechanisms. A study published in the *Proceedings of the National Academy of Sciences* found that nature sounds—such as flowing water and birdsong—significantly reduce stress and enhance mood. Participants reported feeling safer and calmer in natural sound environments, which facilitated psychological restoration. Another study involving more than 7,500 participants found that natural sounds—like birdsong—helped alleviate stress and mental fatigue, especially during pandemic lockdowns, when people became more attuned to the natural sounds around them.

Listening to forest sounds reduces heart rate and promotes feelings of comfort and relaxation compared to urban noise. Nature sounds can enhance cognitive performance and lower arousal levels, contributing to a sense of restoration after stress or fatigue.

Different types of nature sounds offer different benefits. For instance, water sounds are associated with enhanced positive emotions and overall health, while birdsong is particularly effective in reducing anxiety. A study commissioned by the U.S. National Trust found that listening to nature sounds can boost relaxation by 30%—even surpassing the effects of guided meditation apps.

TASTE

Taste signals are routed not only to the gustatory cortex but also to the limbic system, including structures like the amygdala and hippocampus, which are critical for emotional reactions and memory formation. This dual pathway explains why certain flavors can evoke strong emotional responses or awaken deep, long-forgotten memories.

To integrate taste into the garden experience, incorporate plants with edible fruits—not organized into separate areas but interspersed among other plantings so they can be "discovered." These plants should require minimal maintenance and no pesticides (unlike many cultivated species), allowing visitors to pick and eat directly from the plant on the spot. Nothing compares to the taste of a freshly picked fruit and the sense of being nourished directly by nature through such a simple act.

TOUCH

Touch is often considered the most immediate and intimate of the senses. It develops in the womb and remains essential throughout life, influencing emotional bonding and social connection. For example, tactile interactions such as a hug or gentle caress release oxytocin—a hormone linked to bonding and emotional warmth.

In nature, the experience of touch manifests in various forms: the texture of a tree's bark, the sensation of air or water against the skin—experiences that contribute to a sense of grounding and connection. Touch, in particular, invites exploration and curiosity. Contact with different natural surfaces—like the roughness of rocks or the softness of moss— can evoke memories and emotions, making nature feel more familiar and comforting while deepening our connection to it.

BODY AWARENESS

Reconnecting with our body involves a combination of mindfulness, movement, breathing exercises, sensory engagement, and self-reflection. By integrating these practices into daily life, we can cultivate a deeper relationship with our physical selves, leading to enhanced emotional well-being and overall health. Creating a mindful mindset is essential for accessing the healing potential of a garden. Walking through a healing garden can support or even induce a meditative state through its intentional design.

Walking Meditation

Walking meditation is a mindful practice that merges the physical act of walking with meditative awareness, fostering a deeper connection between body and mind. Rooted in Buddhist traditions, it serves as a powerful way to cultivate mindfulness in everyday life. I had the opportunity to practice this for a while in a monastery in Laos. Walking meditation involves moving at a slow, deliberate pace while maintaining awareness of one's surroundings, bodily sensations, and thoughts. Unlike traditional seated meditation, which emphasizes stillness, walking meditation encourages movement and sensory engagement with the environment. Practitioners focus on the sensations of their feet touching the ground, their breath, the shifting of their weight, and the rhythm of their steps—allowing them to remain present in the moment.

Benefits of Walking Meditation

Increased mindfulness: Helps develop present-moment awareness, reducing anxiety and worry.

Mood enhancement: Regular practice supports better emotional regulation and uplifts mood.

Cognitive boost: Mindful walking is linked to improved mental clarity and cognitive function.

Nature connection: Practicing outdoors enhances connection with the natural world, fostering a sense of peace and calm.

Design Elements for a Healing Garden

"So, to truly encounter something means to meet it in a way that goes beyond one's intellectual process. Normally in the West, especially as a scientist—as I am—we are taught to encounter, say, a tree through our concepts: How did this tree's shape arise through the process of natural selection? What forces might have shaped, for instance, the form of its leaves? And you know, it becomes instinctive, when you are a scientist and ecologist, to look at Nature in this way. But that is not a true encounter. A real encounter happens when this conceptual structure dissolves. When you meet the being, as the being, coming from itself, revealing itself to you in a way that transcends your intellect. In a manner that is far more deeply intuitive and much harder to express. In fact, scientific language is inadequate for this kind of encounter. It is poetry that does it. It is a poetic encounter..."

—Dr. Stephan Harding

Creating a garden that acts as a "gateway" for reconnecting with nature and cultivating a deeper inner experience—an immersion similar to what untouched wilderness can offer—requires a synthesis of Western scientific findings, Eastern spiritual approaches, and a cultivated intuitive process, an approach of poetic quality. Such a garden would not only be a place of beauty and function but also an environment that fosters introspection, healing, and spiritual growth, ultimately leading to an initiatory experience of connection:

Maintain Naturalness: Create the sensation of being immersed in nature by using natural elements and materials, along with a design that flows organically. Paths and patterns should mimic natural movement, featuring smooth transitions between spaces. Frederick Law Olmsted famously stated that true artistry in landscape design should be subtle; visitors should not consciously notice the design elements but rather feel immersed in the natural beauty surrounding them.

Create a Sense of "being away": Isolate the garden from human-made elements surrounding the area by creating visual and auditory barriers. If natural views are available, incorporate them as much as possible to extend the garden's sense of place.

Space layout: Provide an enhanced sense of spaciousness and continuously offer new perspectives. Integrate open areas with secluded nooks. Avoid rigid planting schemes and instead focus on creating landscapes with a natural complexity of light and shadow, enhancing the experience of immersion.

Keep Some Elements Hidden: Create a sense of mystery by encouraging exploration and providing varied viewpoints. As visitors walk through labyrinth paths, new points of interest should be gradually revealed. This gentle sense of surprise enhances opportunities for spiritual recovery, reflection, and wonder.

Avoid Attention-Demanding Features: Large, dominant elements that command attention or are visible from afar detract from the engagement of "soft fascination"—the gentle, effortless attention that promotes relaxation and restoration.

Integrate Fractal Design: Incorporate a sense of self-similarity and pattern repetition across different scales in the garden design. Nature is fractal, and maintaining this sense is essential. Create repeating patterns in different scales and use the Fibonacci sequence to guide plant layout and spacing to create a natural rhythm. Integrate spiral patterns that mimic natural forms—but make sure they blend organically into the landscape. Paths should follow free, soft curves rather than straight lines or fixed-radius arcs, creating an organic feel that encourages exploration.

Stimulate All Five Senses: Engaging our senses in natural settings enhances our awareness and appreciation of the environment. By focusing on sensory perceptions, we forge a deeper connection with the natural world, moving beyond merely viewing it as a backdrop for activities.

Hearing: A garden rich in plant biodiversity will attract wildlife and the healing sounds of nature, especially birds and insects, providing them with nourishment and shelter. A water feature, even a small pond with a waterfall, will add a significant auditory dimension with its atmospheric sounds.

Smell: Incorporate plants with pleasant and therapeutic fragrances, ensuring they are accessible for close contact and scent exploration.

Taste: Integrate edible plants throughout the garden rather than segregating them into designated areas. Allow fruits to be "discovered" as one walks. For Mediterranean climates, recommended species include strawberry trees, citrus fruits, pomegranates, figs, mulberries, jujube trees, blackberries, strawberries, and others.

Touch: Ensure that various textures are accessible and inviting to the touch—mosses, stones, bark, and a variety of leaf surfaces.

A gentle slope in the terrain can provide opportunities for mild physical exercise, which strengthens one's connection to the body when combined with a mindful state. Create open spaces for activities such as tai chi, yoga, archery, or other practices encouraging mindfulness and bodily awareness.

Incorporate areas dedicated to planting vegetables and flowers, allowing participants to engage with the cycles of growth and cultivation.

Elements

Paths and Stepping stones

Use natural materials for ground cover and pathways, such as gravel, natural stone, or compacted earth. Stepping stones should be used along certain paths to encourage mindfulness while walking. The design of the stone paths should incorporate irregular arrangements that require visitors to slow down and pay attention to their surroundings. They should not be laid out in straight lines or at uniform heights. The visitor must walk consciously, aiming for the next stone and maintaining a slow pace, all while staying aware of the environment and their bodily movement. The stones should be natural, showing no signs of artificial shaping. Where necessary, stairs can be created using natural stones of similar, suitable thickness. Gently sloping paths offer an opportunity for light physical exercise.

Rocks

"Ishi wo tatten – koto" The art of setting stones

" With these words opens the oldest garden-making treatise in Japan – most likely the oldest in the world – best known by the name Sakuteiki or Records of garden making...... This expression is used to define not only the placement of stones within the garden, but also the act of garden making itself..... How fascinating to see that the simple act of standing a stone upright was so spiritually and aesthetically powerful and so clearly central to the process of making a garden, that the act of setting stones became an appellation for gardening itself."

From the book "Sakuteiki" by Jiro Takei and Marc. P. Keane

The placement of rocks is the most difficult and fascinating aspect of garden creation. It is a foundational and the most permanent element of the garden. First and foremost, rocks must be selected with great care, guided by a mental map of the final desired outcome. They should be chosen from the surface of the ground, whole and unworked. Ensure that they are intact and show no signs of artificial alteration. This authenticity enhances their natural beauty and value. Look for rocks that have developed a patina over time through exposure to wind and water, and those supporting the growth of mosses and lichens. This natural aging process adds character, depth, and a sense of timelessness. Rocks sourced from quarry excavation are generally unsuitable.

The placement of a single rock often determines the layout of the entire space. It must be positioned carefully to enhance the overall aesthetic and functionality of the garden.

I will refer to some of the *Sakuteiki* guidelines for stone placement, avoiding those that involve specific symbolism or cultural significance, as taboos.

- Primary Stones (Shu-seki): Place large, visually dominant stones first as they set the rhythm and design of the garden.
- Secondary Stones (Ju-seki): Arrange supporting stones around the primary ones to strengthen the composition.
- Tertiary Stones (Kyo-seki): Use smaller stones to create balance and fill gaps.

The first stone placed serves as a guide for all that follow, adhering to the *Sakuteiki* principle of "following the desires of the stone" rather than merely arranging them with others. In the *Sakuteiki*, this is literal, as stones are regarded as living entities with a will of their own—here, we may retain its metaphorical meaning.

Identify the "peak" (the highest point), the "face" (the most aesthetically pleasing side), and the "root" (the part to be buried) of each stone. Typically, about one-third or even more of the stone should be buried beneath the surface to achieve stability and the desired visual effect. Each stone's unique form should guide its placement. The arrangement should appear natural, as though the stones are emerging organically from the earth rather than being artificially set.

It is often said that rock arrangements represent natural landscapes, especially in *kare-sansui* gardens. However, I believe that imitating a specific landscape is not the goal; rather, it serves as a mental guide in an otherwise intuitive process of creating something new that feels naturally harmonious and timeless.

Plants

Use native plants to enhance biodiversity and the garden's ecological resilience. Plant them in multiple layers along the pathways to mimic natural ecosystems. Group plants as they would naturally appear in the wild.

Prune only when necessary to maintain a balanced and aesthetically pleasing environment. Choose plants with edible seeds, fruits, and flowers to attract birds and insects. The presence of wildlife is vital in a healing garden.

Instead of a conventional lawn, which often looks artificial, consider creating a meadow to create open, cool, walkable areas. Meadows are more beautiful, filled with a variety of subtle wildflowers and shades of green. They promote biodiversity and are aesthetically richer, changing with the seasons and years.

Trees are naturally the most important plants in a garden. But moderation is key: make sure they do not dominate the entire space. The richest, most biodiverse, and most beautiful landscapes are those transitional edges between forests and meadows, where trees are visible but sparse, allowing the environment to remain open and inviting.

Dense tree plantings can create environments that feel less welcoming.

Water

Even a small pond with a waterfall can have a profound impact on the garden experience. It creates a powerful ambient soundscape. Keep the water feature alive with plants and small fish, creating a tiny ecosystem that will attract birds, insects, and even small mammals, further boosting the garden's biodiversity.

If even that is not possible, a small basin with flowing water will suffice.

In psychoanalysis, water is considered a primary symbol of the unconscious. Jung described it as a reservoir of repressed experiences, emotions, collective memories, and untapped potential. Water bodies symbolize the vastness and depth of the subconscious, suggesting that while we may see the surface (our conscious thoughts), the deeper layers remain hidden and complex.

Water is associated with intuition and dreams, acting as a gateway to deeper feelings and unresolved issues. Dreams featuring water encourage individuals to explore their subconscious emotions, memories, and desires.

In Zen practice, water symbolizes the fluid and ever-changing nature of reality. Just as water flows and adapts to its environment, Zen teachings emphasize the importance of accepting change and uncertainty in life. Ponds are also seen as mirrors that reflect the self. The calmness of a pond invites introspection and reflection.

A small pond can have a large impact.

Color

Avoid bold hues that demand attention or large expanses of uniformly colored flowers that dominate the landscape. Such displays prevent the engagement of *soft fascination*, which gently draws people in, allowing for reflection and introspection.

Subtle flower shades scattered throughout the garden, the varied greens, and the rich colors of autumn are ideal.

Lines

Avoid straight lines or strict geometric curves in pathways, plantings, and garden elements.

Avoid hard, clean edges in general; prefer soft transitions. Use freely flowing curves, fractal forms, and (sparingly) unexpected turns to create a natural feeling.

Accessories

Garden accessories such as seating, steps, bridges, water basins, etc., should be made from natural materials. Whenever possible, use a suitable stone or tree trunk for seating. A moss-covered stone construction could be a beautiful addition.

Plastic and shiny metal are forbidden—they are psychological and aesthetic pollutants.

Wood (unvarnished) and stone are ideal materials.

Attention to Detail

Details matter—you are asked to "see the universe in a grain of sand." Thus, even seemingly minor elements, such as lichens on a trunk, a stone placed perfectly, or a tiny plant emerging from a crack, must be given careful attention, especially in spaces designed for sitting and contemplation, where visitors can observe them. They exert their influence even if not consciously perceived—just as Olmsted noted, they directly affect our subconscious.

Within a Healing Garden

"On a mountain path,

A single stone rests alone—

The world holds its breath."

Haiku by Yosa Buson

Let us take a walk through a small garden that follows most of the guiding principles of a healing garden.

It is a home garden on a 5,000 square-meter plot, close to the city, yet isolated from the rather densely populated surroundings thanks to the slopes of a small valley in which it is nestled.

It is surrounded by the natural and rural landscape. No other residence or human structure is visible except for a neighboring house, from which it is effectively isolated by dense planting of trees and shrubs in successive layers.

A dirt road through the forest, with no traffic, leads to the house. Nevertheless, a buffer zone has been left, covered with maquis shrubs and pines, growing freely between the house and the road to further isolate the home from it.

Although it is only ten minutes from the city, there is a profound sense of "remoteness." The somewhat adventurous journey along the narrow dirt road and through the forest creates the feeling that you are traveling to a hidden, faraway place.

Open and secluded spaces are interconnected within the garden through freely flowing paths and passages. Masses of vegetation define the spaces and control the views from each point, creating a sense of natural complexity.

The destination of the paths is hidden—a narrow trail through the vegetation will lead to a new, unexpected space, creating a sense of anticipation and mystery. The visitor never has a complete view of the site, and there are no dominant reference points.

Fractality:

The rounded shape is repeated at different scales, from the small stones in the foreground, to the low shrubs, the tall hedges, and the distant trees.

Fractality: The slope of the hillside is repeated at four different scales with zones of vegetation, extending to the clusters near the house and also reflected on the opposite side.

The Senses

The place is isolated from urban sounds thanks to the slopes of the valley, covered with pine forest and maquis vegetation. There are moments when you can "hear the silence," as one visitor put it. The sounds of nature dominate — birds singing over the background whisper of the wind through the trees, accompanied by the rhythmic section of cicadas and crickets.

The garden is planted mostly with native aromatic plants and more. You will encounter fragrant plants in almost every corner of the garden, integrated into clusters and hedges: oregano, rosemary, lavender, bay laurel, mastic trees, dittany, sage, artemisia, basil, and some wild species like fennel (Foeniculum vulgare). They are accessible for touching and smelling — a parade of scents.

The garden offers small snacks during most seasons of the year, from plants integrated into the design of the plant groupings: strawberry trees (Arbutus unedo) and citrus fruits in autumn and winter, loquats in late winter, mulberries in early spring, apricots at the beginning of summer, and later figs, jujubes, and pomegranates at the end of summer. Small snacks, picked directly from the plants.

Interesting textures are also available for touching and easily accessible: bark, rounded stones, and the soft fur of the cats and dogs that roam and bring life to the garden.

Spaces for exercise are created. The lawn in front of the house is designed so that a small group can practice Tai Chi, and a little further away, in an open clearing surrounded by forest, there is a larger area with enough space for free play and archery targets.

Climbing trees and exploring the nearby forest are also available options.

A small vegetable garden creates an opportunity for direct contact with the soil, exercise, and seasonal vegetable snacks.

This is a small, organically managed vegetable garden combined with a chicken coop. All residues from the lawn and plants are recycled in the chicken coop together with organic kitchen waste. The chickens, which are the best compost producers, eat and mix the organic material and also enrich it with the necessary nitrogenous matter. The resulting compost is used in the vegetable garden and the fruit trees.

Biodiversity: The planting of native plants, the selective preservation of wild plant species, and the proximity to the forest create conditions for the presence of numerous insects, birds, and small mammals. Large buzzards patrol over the valley, a flock of wild pigeons takes off every morning from the nearby forest, while jays are regular visitors to the garden, pecking at the fruits of the trees. The small pond attracts hedgehogs, many small birds, dragonflies, and other insects. Every winter, robins decorate it. The wild Phoeniculum (wild fennel) is allowed to grow freely because it hosts the caterpillars of Papilio Machaon, the large black-and-white butterfly, which thus decorates the garden for much of the year.

The walking paths are paved with river pebbles and natural stones. The river pebbles consist of stones of various sizes and colors, a natural material. The stepping stones are natural and unprocessed, of different sizes and slightly varying heights, creating an irregular arrangement.

The steps are made with natural stones of similar suitable thickness. They are placed so as to blend into the adjacent group of rocks, creating a harmonious whole.

The rocks are used to create a retaining feature for the slope of a steep hillside, incorporating a small pond and the steps.

Under construction, indicating the setting of the rocks.

The rocks were chosen to have developed a patina over time due to exposure to wind and water, as well as the presence of mosses and lichens. They were transported and placed with special care to avoid being broken or scratched.

Once the plants have grown, the entire arrangement takes on a sense of having always been there as part of the natural landscape.

A rock with a flat top is the only way to pass from the veranda to the garden. It is beautiful but not very convenient, thus creating an element that facilitates, yet at the same time, makes the transition from the house to the garden somewhat demanding in effort. An element borrowed from Japanese gardens, this rock both separates and connects, imbuing the act of moving from the house to the garden with a certain significance.

The pond with the waterfall, although tiny, is an important feature of the garden. First of all, the sound of the waterfall creates an atmosphere throughout much of the garden where it can be heard. It provides a sense of coolness during our hot Mediterranean summer. It is also a magnet for wildlife, as it is the only water source in the area. It offers an invitation for relaxation and contemplation. It is hypnotic in a magical way. A visitor has named the bench overlooking the lake the "meditation bench."

Plants

The garden is planted mainly with native plants, enhancing biodiversity and animating the garden with wildlife.

Hedge with: Pistacia lentiscus, Oreganum Vulgare, Rosmarinus officinalis, Arbutus unedo, Viburnum tinus, Vitex agnus-castus, Pyracantha coccinea, Phoeniculum vulgare, single petal Rose.

Clipped small trees: Myrtus communis and Quercus coccifera. Although kept small in size, they are old, and their trunks are weathered and covered in lichen, creating a sense of timelessness and of being inside an old forest.

Ground cover: a small "meadow" instead of a conventional lawn that doesn't require chemicals, changes with the seasons and years, and offers small wildflowers and different shades of green. It's not a one-dimensional traditional lawn but a small, evolving ecosystem that enhances biodiversity. Bees and butterflies adorn it and bring it to life.

Colors: colors are subtle, creating a mood without dominating or demanding attention.

Spring

Winter

Fall

Details

Epilogue

A Garden for Connection is, above all, an intermediate space. It is neither pure nature nor alienated civilization. To create an experience of initiation, it must evoke a sense of sacredness-a feeling of respect and appreciation for nature. It is a "gateway," and like all gateways to the sacred (both inner and outer), it is low; one must bow with respect and humility to pass through, just like in a tea garden. The garden itself is humble-nothing spectacular or ostentatious dominates. The "naturalness" we seek does not mean the garden should be messy. It requires careful and consistent maintenance, which is an art and an initiatory process in itself. Shrubs must be regularly and carefully pruned, and weeds selectively removed. Wild plants that harmoniously integrate into the garden are allowed to grow. In this way, the garden changes and evolves over time. Sick plants must be treated or replaced. We cannot use chemicals to combat pests or fertilizers. Doing so would reduce the biodiversity we so desire and likely create health problems for the users. The effort to maintain the garden in this way is also a healing process, and because this is reflected in the result, it enhances its effect.

Despite the effort put into maintaining the garden, care must be taken so it does not appear overly artificial. Our interventions discreetly guide nature rather than imposing upon it forcefully. Everything is carefully considered but appears natural—the teacher is nature itself. The final result must seem natural in the sense that it is perfectly imperfect. The Japanese concept of wabi-sabi, which embraces transience and imperfection and sees beauty in them, creates the magical combination and balance of culture and nature achieved by Japanese gardens. This is a shared effort on your part; let nature do its own and follow it with appreciation and respect.

A Short Story from the Orient

Before the tea ceremony, the tea garden and tea house are carefully prepared to be in perfect condition to welcome guests. The garden's preparation symbolizes not only physical cleanliness but also a spiritual readiness for the tea ceremony. It is a meditative experience and an integral part of the entire ritual of the Tea Ceremony.

Thus, the apprentice of the chanoyu master prepares the garden. He places fresh water in the tsukubai, washes the stones and slabs, tends the moss, and cleans the garden of fallen leaves and twigs. When he finishes, the tea master comes to inspect, but from his expression, it is clear he is not satisfied with the result. So the apprentice resumes work, washing the stones and slabs again and carefully cleaning every small fallen leaf he may have missed, leaving the garden sparkling clean and tidy. The tea master returns for inspection but still is not pleased. He approaches a small tree and gently shakes it so that some leaves fall and scatter across the garden. Then he steps back, looks at the garden, and says, "Now it is perfect," before leaving to invite the guest into the garden.

References

1. Carl G. Jung: "Dream Analysis: Notes of the Seminar Given in 1928-1930" 1984 Princeton University Press
2. Carl G. Jung: "The Earth Has a Soul" Edited by Meredith Sabini 2002 North Atlantic Books
3. Erich Fromm: "The Sane Society"1955 Rinehart & Company
4. Susan Sontag: "The Aesthetic of Silence"1967 Published in the collection "Styles of Radical Will" by Farrar, Straus and Giroux
5. Erich Fromm, Richard J. DeMartino, D.T. Suzuki: "Psychoanalysis and Zen Buddhism" 1960 Harper & Row
6. Joseph Henderson: "The Way of the Dream"1988 Shambhala Publications
7. Guy Debord: "The Society of the Spectacle"1967 Buchet-Chastel (original French edition)
8. Edward O. Wilson: "Biophilia"1984 Harvard University Press
9. Roger Ulrich: "Biophilic Theory and Research for Healthcare Design" 2008 In "Biophilic Design: The Theory, Science, and Practice of Bringing Buildings to Life" by Wiley
10. Oliver Sacks: "Everything in Its Place: First Loves and Last Tales" 2019 Alfred A. Knopf
11. Stephen and Rachel Kaplan: "The Experience of Nature: A Psychological Perspective" 1989 Cambridge University Press
12. Frederick Law Olmsted: "Civilizing American Cities: Writings on City Landscapes" Da Capo Press
13. Florence Williams: "The Nature Fix": 2017 W.W. Norton & Company
14. F. Stephen Mayer, Cynthia McPherson Frantz: "The Connectedness to Nature Scale: A Measure of Individuals' Feeling in Community with Nature" 2004 Journal of Environmental Psychology

15. EunYeong Choe, Anna Jorgensen, David Sheffield: "Does a Natural Environment Enhance the Effectiveness of Mindfulness-Based Stress Reduction (MBSR)? Examining the Mental Health and Wellbeing, and Nature Connectedness Benefits" 2020 Landscape and Urban Planning
16. Stephan Harding: "Gaia Alchemy: The Reuniting of Science, Psyche, and Soul" 2022 Bear & Company
17. Eugen Herrigel: "Zen in the Art of Archery" 1948 Routledge & Kegan Paul
18. Jiro Takei & Marc P. Keane: "Sakuteiki: Visions of the Japanese Garden" 2001 Tuttle Publishing
19. Abd al-Hayy Moore: "Zen Rock Gardening" 1999 Tuttle Publishing
20. Fotis Terzakis: "Against the sun's direction" Book B 2015 Panoptikon
21. Preston M. Houser, Mizuno Katsuhiko: "Invitation to Tea Gardens"1992 Mitsumura Suiko Shoin Co. (on page 38 and 39)
22. Kazuko Okakura: "The Book of Tea" 1906 Fox Duffield & Company
23. Yoshifumi Miyazaki: "Shinrin Yoku: The Japanese Art of Forest Bathing" 2018 Timber Press
24. Richard Taylor: "Fractal Expressionism—Where Art Meets Science" 2003 Leonardo
25. Qing Li: "Forest Bathing: How Trees Can Help You Find Health and Happiness" 2018 Viking

www.ingramcontent.com/pod-product-compliance
Lightning Source LLC
Chambersburg PA
CBHW051539120626
46551CB00013B/1298